The First Albertans

The stones are not mute.

They tell of successive cultures, lives and trading patterns of an Alberta long ago

...of a microlith technology that produced blades sharper than surgical steel

...of a world of the spirit recorded in ancient medicine wheels

...and they hint at an ice-free corridor through Alberta that may have peopled the Americas.

This, and much more, awaits your discovery in *The First Albertans*.

The First Albertans

An Archaeological Search

Gail Helgason

LONE
PINE

The Publishers:
Lone Pine Publishing
414, 10357 109 Street
Edmonton, Alberta
T5J 1N3

Typesetting by Pièce de Résistance Typographers, Edmonton

Printed by Commercial Colour Press Ltd., Edmonton

Canadian Cataloguing in Publication Data

Helgason, Gail, 1950-
    The First Albertans
    —An Archaeological Search

    Bibliography: p. 220
    ISBN 0-919433-19-7

    1. Man, Prehistoric - Alberta. 2 Archaeology -
Alberta. I. Archaeological Survey of Alberta.
II. Title.
E78.A34H44 1987   971.23   C87-091218-6

58,121

Cover illustration: Don Inman

Publisher's Acknowledgements

The First Albertans is the result of an initiative taken by Paul
Donahue, former director of the Archaeological Survey of Alberta,
who first approached Lone Pine Publishing with the idea for a book
that would enrich Western Canada's cultural base with a generally
understandable record of its known archaeological sites. The idea
was further championed by his successor, Jack Ives, who contributed hugely with time, knowledge and talent to its realization.
Martin Magne, Head of Research with the ASA, also deserves particular credit for his exceptional contribution in the coordination of
manuscript production.

Lone Pine Publishing gratefully acknowledges the assistance of
the Archaeological Survey of Alberta, Alberta Culture, the Canada
Council; and, the Canadian Department of Communications in the
production of this book.

Acknowledgement

This, the first book about Alberta archaeology written for a general readership, was initiated by the Archaeological Survey of Alberta (Historical Resources Division, Alberta Culture). My own involvement as the second writer began in September, 1986, barely three months before first drafts were due. Only through the cooperation of all those concerned were deadlines met. I am most grateful to Jack Ives, Director of the Archaeological Survey of Alberta (ASA), Grant Kennedy, President of Lone Pine Publishing, Martin Magne, Head of Research with the ASA (on whom much of the burden of coordinating manuscript production fell), and my excellent and understanding editor, Jim Scott. Each made unique and valuable contributions to *The First Albertans*.

Thanks as well to ASA staff, who cheerfully contributed their expertise and detailed editorial advice: Bruce Ball (for information on parklands), Alwynne Beaudoin (palaeoenvironments), Jack Brink (Head-Smashed-In and Plains), Heather Devine (educational programs), Michael Forsman (historic period), Karie Hardie (for multitudinous errands), Wendy Johnson (drafting), Heinz Pyszczyk (historic period), Brian Ronaghan (Eastern Slopes), Rod Vickers (Plains), Milt Wright (Head-Smashed-In and boreal forest), John Priegert (for assistance with research materials), and Lois Schneider and Martina Purdon (for last minute errands and voluminous photocopying).

Bill Williams deserves credit for getting the project started and for providing valuable research material from which this book is drawn.

Don Inman created superlative illustrations. Charles Schweger provided expertise on palaeoecology, Nat Rutter on the ice-free corridor, Michael Wilson on megafauna, Darryl Fedje on Vermilion Lakes, Jim Burns on Pleistocene/Holocene fauna, and Tom Andrews on northern life. Thanks also to Lone Pine Publishing staff: Yuet C. Chan (design and layout), and Raymond Gariépy (final edit).

Finally, thanks to my husband, John Dodd, who contributed invaluable editorial advice, and much-needed moral support.

Thomas Carlyle wrote that, "The tragedy in life is not what men suffer, but what they miss."

This book will have attained its goal if, in only a small way, it opens the reader's imagination to another dimension of Alberta's past which they may have missed — that occupied by prehistoric Albertans.

Gail Helgason

Author's Preface

This book is about searching, not only for the first Albertans, but also for a deeper understanding of all the peoples who inhabited Alberta long before this province had a name.

Hunters and gatherers around the world lived a successful way of life for 40,000 years before the introduction of agriculture and, much later, the industrial revolution. In Alberta, the ancestors of today's native people learned to do much more than merely survive for thousands of years in a landscape which Europeans, in historic times, were to find brutal and in some cases, uninhabitable. Yet, so much of the way of life of prehistoric Albertans is lost to us. Archaeology holds the best key to illuminating the mysterious lives of long ago.

To search implies to discover; it also implies to question. Readers hoping to find neat, chronological answers about the peoples of ancient Alberta will find more queries here than solutions. It is precisely an attitude of lively inquiry about the past which the Archaeological Survey of Alberta hopes, with this book, to encourage among an interested and informed public.

Readers will also find a determined attempt to place Alberta archaeology in a broad continental and international context. Cultures do not change in isolation from each other; the challenge of archaeology is to piece together the cultural dynamics of the past.

Some may also find in this book a few surprises about what archaeology is about. Archaeology, of all the social sciences, is perhaps the most prone to misconception and stereotype. No swashbuckling pyramid explorers will surface on these pages, only diligent scientists whose work may involve paper and pen as much as shovel and trowel.

Much is yet to be discovered...
and to those who will pursue those discoveries
we dedicate this book.

Contents

The rich past of Alberta's first inhabitants is found on the land they touched.

1

Two Worlds Meet

History — as we usually think of it — came to the Canadian northwest barely 200 years ago. The first Europeans to venture that far west and north, such as Anthony Henday and Peter Pond, brought it with them. They had the written word and they used it to keep their journals and accounts. Strangers to that wilderness, they made a written record of their whereabouts, as best they could reckon it.

And so history began in Alberta! But the fur traders did not arrive in an empty land. Henday, Pond and their followers, who measured the passing of time by the less than 2,000 years since the birth of Christ, at once encountered people who had perhaps lived on the same lands for 10,000 years or more. They were called Indians.

Those Native North Americans did not possess the written word, therefore, much of their past is lost in time. Alberta archaeology, as this book hopes to demonstrate, can help to retrieve part of their fascinating story.

The extent of the unwritten past of our human ancestors in comparison with what we call *history* is difficult to comprehend. It helps to use the metaphor of a day, twenty-four hours representing the time people have lived on the earth. If it is midnight now, the fur trade came to the northwest six seconds ago, and King John signed the Magna Carta twenty-two seconds ago. Jesus of Nazareth was born at fifty-seven seconds before midnight. Alexander the Great established his empire one minute and seven seconds ago. Written language was developed two minutes and twenty seconds ago. Native people probably first came to Alberta about six minutes ago. Everything before 11:57 p.m. — more than ninety-nine per cent of humanity's past — predates history.

Before the fur traders, two different cultures, on two different continents, had existed for thousands of years on what might have been two separate planets. The Europeans had their written languages and their increasingly-technological society. The aboriginal people of the Canadian northwest had a sophisticated, viable society based on hunting and gathering, a way of life that goes back at least 40,000 years. Both achieved success in their own worlds.

Native society was based on hunting and gathering.

With the arrival of the fur traders, and the earlier arrival of trade goods through Cree intermediaries, the way of life of one of those societies would begin to be transformed. The thousands of years of what we call prehistory, the past before written language, had ended in the Canadian northwest.

Who were the smooth-faced, dark-skinned people of the northwest? Where did they come from? To Pond, Henday and some of the other fur traders who followed, those questions were intriguing, but of secondary importance. Furs and fortunes evoked their paramount interest. Immense territories full of sleek fur-bearing animals awaited exploration and exploitation; great profits could be realized by being the only trader in an area of abundant furs.

Like most great events, this one began quietly enough. Perhaps it started in the clear, cold water of a small stream above Lac La Loche, in what is now northwestern Saskatchewan. The water ran so shallow the summer of 1778, that Pond, an independent trader from Connecticut, and his French-Canadian voyageurs were forced to half-drag their four canoes along the creek bed. Finally, it dried up completely.

Pond's men had no choice but to portage. Sweating and straining under the load of canoes, provisions and trade goods, the small fur-trading brigade struggled uphill through thick pine and spruce. All day, they laboured up a long rise of land, later known as Thirteen-Mile-Carrying Place. Eight steep hills had to be conquered.

At last the group reached its destination, the summit now known as Methy Portage. From the high bank, about fifteen kilometres east of the present-day Saskatchewan-Alberta border, Pond gazed down at the beautiful Clearwater River. Unlike any other river the fur traders had yet found, the Clearwater flowed westwards. The panorama across its wide, forested valley extended more than sixty kilometres into Alberta. All Pond's fur-trading instincts must have told him that he was entering the richest fur-bearing region on the continent.

Pond could not have known it, but with his conquest of Methy Portage, the history of Western Canada was about to reach a crossroads. The Yankee trader had discovered the crucial inland route linking the fur-hungry markets of Europe with the fur-rich Canadian northwest.

Once Pond entered the Clearwater Basin, he breached the natural defence that had sheltered the Indians of the northwest from Europeans who had arrived in the east more than 250 years before. They were among the last Native North Americans to come into contact with European culture.

The Pace of Change Accelerates

At the time Pond stood at Methy Summit, white traders for the Hudson Bay's Company had not ventured this far northwest. Instead, they depended on Cree middlemen for the costly transportation of furs to company forts at Cumberland House in Saskatchewan and York Factory on Hudson Bay. The Natives who lived in the Athabasca region of Alberta had already received guns, metal pots and other European goods through the Cree. But it is unlikely any had yet seen a white face.

All that was about to change. Pond was the first known white person to find a connection between the Hudson Bay drainage system and the Athabasca and Arctic drainage systems. The same route would soon be travelled by other fur traders and explorers, including Alexander Mackenzie and David Thompson.

We do not know Pond's thoughts as he looked upon the vista from Methy Summit. The portion of his journal covering his years in the northwest was used in the nineteenth century to fuel a stove in the kitchen of a Connecticut governor.

But historical records tell us that Pond constructed the first fur trade post in Alberta later the same year, on the Athabasca River, sixty kilometres south of huge Lake Athabasca. (Archaeologists have yet to find any traces of the post.) In 1779, Pond and other independent traders formed the rival North West Company which embarked on fierce competition with the Hudson's Bay Company in the Athabasca and Saskatchewan regions. The strategy of the new company — to bypass the Cree middlemen by buying the best furs directly from the Natives in the interior — would bring both companies, with their forts and their European ways, headlong into the wilderness that became Alberta.

Before Alberta's History Came Prehistory

Pond reputedly drew his first map of the Canadian northwest in a Quebec bar while on a search for money to finance his western trading schemes. A map (even if wildly inaccurate) would surely impress the fur merchants of the town. Nonetheless, Pond was the first to map and explore the Canadian northwest, although he was not the first white man to penetrate what we now call Alberta. Anthony Henday probably visited the southern and central parts of the province in 1754-55.

The history of Alberta, however, predates both Henday and

14

Pond. In the York Factory Journal for June 12, 1715, Henry Kelsey wrote of a Cree trader named Swan: "... he brought a sample of that gum or pitch that flows out of the banks of that river as I mentioned."

Here is history's first mention of Alberta. Fittingly, it described the northeastern oil sands, which Natives used to mend canoes. Later, the oil sands were identified as one of the largest reservoirs of oil trapped within the earth's crust.

History, it seems, came later to Alberta than to most parts of North America. But the written word is a relative newcomer to all human societies. Although the human race has existed for hundreds of thousands of years (some say as much as three million), the written word did not appear before 3,000 B.C. Until recently, literacy has been a skill slow to spread.

Without written words to illuminate the story of the first people to occupy this province, we must learn to "read" the clues they left behind — their stone weapons, bone tools, medicine wheels, rock paintings, stone cairns, tipi rings and other signposts. We must look to archaeology.

Bits of Bone, Chips of Stone

A worker fixing a sewer line beneath the city of Lethbridge found a sharp stone shaped like a spear tip. A farmer cultivating a field near Grande Prairie came across large bison bones from an extinct species of buffalo. A fire lookout warden happened on a strange circle of stones on a mountain ledge in the Eastern Slopes.

These discoveries, and many similar ones, are the beacons of the past. The find by the Lethbridge sewer worker, for example, was dated by Alberta archaeologists as a stone weapon more than 10,000-years-old.

The job of archaeologists is to study human cultures of the past, largely through material objects or debris found at locations (or *sites*) once occupied by humans. Anything made by humans, including flakes or by-products from stone tool manufacture, is called an *artifact*. The sum of human traces from any particular site or region is called the *archaeological record*.

Although archaeology encompasses the time from the first evidence of human activity to the present, the major focus in Alberta is on prehistoric times. Here, the archaeological

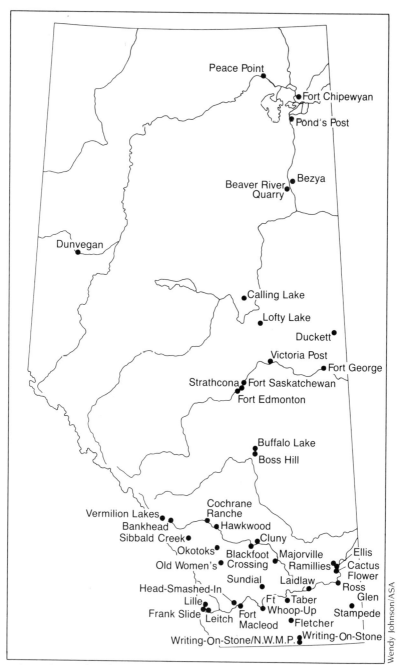

Peace Point

Fort Chipewyan

Pond's Post

Bezya

Beaver River
Quarry

Dunvegan

Calling Lake

Lofty Lake

Duckett

Victoria Post

Fort George

Strathcona Fort Saskatchewan

Fort Edmonton

Buffalo Lake

Boss Hill

Cochrane
Ranche

Vermilion Lakes

Hawkwood

Bankhead

Sibbald Creek

Cluny

Okotoks

Blackfoot
Crossing

Majorville

Ellis

Old Women's

Ramillies

Cactus
Flower

Sundial

Laidlaw

Ross

Head-Smashed-In

Glen

Lille

Ft
Whoop-Up

Taber

Frank Slide

Leitch

Fort
Macleod

Fletcher

Stampede

Writing-On-Stone/N.W.M.P.

Writing-On-Stone

Wendy Johnson/ASA

Locations of archaeological sites in Alberta which are noted in
the text.

record is far from complete. No one knows how many archaeological sites Alberta contains — to date, approximately 17,000 prehistoric sites have been recorded. There may be a million or more undiscovered sites.

Not all areas of the province were equally occupied in prehistoric times, but they were all peopled at one time or another. Archaeologists who have studied the plains of southern Alberta say it is difficult in some places not to find an archaeological site every thirty metres or so, if only a bit of stone from prehistoric tool manufacture. Sheltered river valleys, such as those of the Oldman, the Bow, the Red Deer and the North Saskatchewan, show signs of occupation for thousands of years. Edmonton and Calgary, for instance, were both inhabited in prehistoric times.

As recently as the 1960s, some archaeologists believed prehistoric people had never occupied Alberta's Rocky Mountains. A vast amount of archaeological work since then has resulted in a completely different view. Recent road construction on the Trans-Canada Highway near Banff townsite, for example, gives evidence of human habitation dating back more than 10,000 years. Although the archaeology of the southern plains has been relatively well explored, considerably more research is needed to understand prehistoric life in the Eastern Slopes and the northern forests.

Alberta Archaeology — What It Is and Is Not

When many North Americans think of archaeology, they envisage pyramids and Minoan frescoes. Such well-chronicled glories are the realm of *classical* archaeology.

The term refers to the archaeology of Mediterranean countries such as Greece, Italy, Sicily and North Africa. It began with Heinrich Schliemann, a German grocer's son who, working from Homer's epic poem, set out in 1871 to find the city of Troy. Schliemann's search led him to a site called Hissarlik in northwestern Turkey. Although experts today would not agree that the level of occupation at Hissarlik, which Schliemann called Troy, was in fact the city, they do agree that one of the levels at this site is indeed Homer's Troy.

Schliemann's careful excavation methods ultimately proved far more important than his discovery of Troy, however, for

17

they led to the founding of archaeology. Budding archaeologists rushed from all points of the compass to the Mediterranean to seek out those treasures of the ancients that the world had only known by literature.

The classical school of archaeology which Schliemann founded is closely linked to classical literature such as the *Iliad* and the *Odyssey*. The understanding of ancient languages, such as Greek, Latin and Hittite, is thus vital to the pursuit of this discipline. Indeed, classical archaeology is really more related to the humanities than to social science. It includes the appreciation of works of art by individual artists — for example, the statue of Aphrodite, made by Praxiteles for dedication at Olympia.

If archaeology were confined solely to exploring pyramids, looking for buried cities and temples or examining artwork on urns, the archaeology of Alberta would indeed be slowgoing. Obviously, we have no pyramids; there is no chance of discovering ancient buried cities. The pottery of prehistoric Alberta, it must be admitted, is gray and little adorned.

Archaeology can, however, be conceived of in another way altogether. Its goal can be defined as *understanding how people lived in the past*, whether or not they dwelled in or near the Mediterranean world.

This broader approach to archaeology, which this book is concerned with, is actually a subdiscipline of *anthropology* — the science dealing with the origin, development and customs of humans. Physical anthropology is concerned with the physiological evolution of humans; cultural anthropology deals with human social development, beliefs and practices; and linguistic anthropology deals with issues of language.

James Deetz, professor of Anthropology at Brown University offers the following definition of the goals of archaeology:

> Archaeologists are anthropologists who usually excavate the material remains of past cultures, and through the study of such evidence, attempt to recreate the history of man from his earliest past and to determine the nature of cultural systems at different times and places around the world.

Archaeology, then, applies the concepts of anthropology, the natural sciences, history and philosophy to try and gain understanding of the human past and how cultural development occurred through time. To pursue this kind of inquiry, archaeologists study the *material remains* of past human life. They do not merely study artifacts; far more important is the context in which artifacts are found and their relationship with each other. Indeed, few archaeologists are great collectors themselves. The value of any spear point or pot fragment is not in the object itself, but in the understanding it can offer about the life of past cultures.

Anthropological archaeology, moreover, includes the study of material remains from all past societies in the world, simple or complex. It encompasses the time period beginning with the first evidence of human activity to the recent past; some archaeologists even study today's garbage.

If Albertans wish to harness archaeology to look into the prehistoric past, they must be prepared to learn from an archaeological record more subtle, but no less profound, than that of the classicists. The rewards are there, if only we can adjust our vision.

"There are enormous physical manifestations out on the landscape that are almost the equivalent of Stonehenges and pyramids, but they just don't all stand up in one place and make a big structure," says Jack Brink, senior archaeologist with the provincial government's Archaeological Survey of Alberta.

"But in terms of the human labor and engineering, we can show you things that are the equivalent of that, in my opinion."

The people who occupied Alberta in prehistoric times were hunters and gatherers — nomadic bands who perhaps moved up to fifty times a year. That wandering way of life stands in contrast to settlement patterns in Eastern North America or the Pacific Northwest, where fairly large semi-permanent or seasonal villages developed in prehistoric times, along with agriculture or specialized salmon harvesting.

Nomadic hunters, by definition, have not marked the landscape with anything like the glories of classical archaeology — the walled towns and great halls of Troy or Greece, the Mesopotamian civilizations, or the spectacular remains of ancient Egypt. Nor have they left the sizeable, complex burial mounds or stockaded villages which archaeologists find in some parts of North America. Hunters and gatherers touch lightly on the land.

The lightness of their archaeological legacy, however, must

not be mistaken for lack of complexity or ingenuity. Ancient Alberta hunters designed complex antelope traps and snowshoes; they constructed large ceremonial rock features and painted evocative rock art. They established a successful way of life which withstood a severe and changeable climate for thousands of years.

Square by Square: How Archaeologists Map the Past

The twin aims of anthropological archaeology are to study "culture process" and "culture history." Culture process is concerned with how and why cultures operated as they did in the past, and how they came to change. Such a study, in attempting to explain variations in human behaviour, must also focus on the overlap between different systems or patterns of human cultures.

Culture history builds up a chronological framework for the events and processes of the past. For example, Plains archaeologists are interested in finding out when nomadic bands first used the bow and arrow or learned how to make pottery. They look for chronology: the sequence of past events and their relationship to one another.

A technique called *stratigraphic excavation* is the primary method for achieving chronological data. The basis is simple: sediments are deposited in layers, with the lowest layer the oldest. Before excavating, archaeologists mark off the site with a grid. As layers of earth are carefully peeled away, the precise location of each item is noted, layer by layer, square by square. It is not unusual to find literally thousands of stone flakes within a few metres.

If artifacts are found in *stratigraphic context* — that is, in the same layer they were originally laid — it may be possible to date each layer. Archaeologists are as interested in the pattern of artifacts as the artifacts themselves. People bring archaeologists shoeboxes full of fragments found all over the countryside, but that is of limited use to them if they don't know precisely where they were found. The arrangement of bison bones at a site, for example, can give clues to which areas were used for butchering or hide preparation. We can thus gain a glimpse into the daily life of prehistoric people.

Organic materials, such as bone or charcoal, can be dated

by a technique called *radiocarbon dating*. This method is based on the rate of decay of the radioactive isotope C-14 which is found in organic matter. Theoretically, the method allows scientists to work out the absolute age of organic material at time of death, but comparison between historical dates and radiocarbon dates in Egypt, for example, have shown lack of correlation. Recently, scientists have confirmed the discrepancy by the radiocarbon dating of tree rings of a known age (called dendrochronology). Scientists now believe the production of C-14 varied somewhat throughout time, and that radiocarbon dates should be matched with tree ring dates to achieve a more accurate date. When dating organic material, archaeologists include a range for error, perhaps of several hundreds or thousands of years.

One of the challenges of Alberta archaeology is dealing with a record often plentiful in quantity yet sparse in variety. In Mesopotamia, people worked gold as far back as 5,000 years ago. Cave paintings in France date from 15,000 years ago; fine ceramics appeared in the Far East at least 3,000 years ago. Archaeologists who study nomadic people in North America have far fewer clues to draw from. You could say the detective story is more challenging over here.

ASA

The Fletcher site in southern Alberta—an example of stratigraphy.

Alberta Tools for Archaeological Detectives

The archaeological record in Alberta is limited to three broad categories: stone, bone and ceramic artifacts. This record is supplemented by information about past environments, or *palaeoenvironmental* data. The challenge facing Alberta archaeology is to fully plumb the few clues provided.

Stone• Skillfully flaked flint *projectile points* — the sharp stone pieces prehistoric people placed at the tips of spears, darts and arrows — are characteristic of the hunters of North America. In Alberta, with the absence of permanent prehistoric dwellings, vast artwork or other clues in the archaeological record, these points and the *flakes* (by-products from their manufacture), take on great importance. They are the vital foundation of the archaeological record of this province.

Projectile points come in many shapes and sizes, and are made from a variety of raw materials. Some appear crudely shaped while others are refined and aesthetically pleasing. Classifying or grouping artifacts according to type is called *typology*, and is a mainstay of the study of archaeology.

Some North American archaeologists are preoccupied with arranging types of points in a series showing change, and have produced detailed chronologies based upon this classification. They might argue, for example, that a person who produced a delicately-made Avonlea point belonged to the Avonlea culture. Other archaeologists are extremely wary of equating points with people, or of inferring marked differences between cultures based on the difference of one millimetre in the width of a point. Neither point of view can yet be proven right or wrong.

Even though the significance of different point styles is not fully understood, archaeologists can still learn much from stone weapons and their manufacture. Much of their knowledge is gleaned from understanding the principles of stone tool-making. Archaeologists refer to stone tool-making as a *reductive process* because it involves removing stone or *lithic* material from a larger piece of stone. This is accomplished in two ways, either by chipping and flaking, or by a process of grinding and finishing.

Prehistoric hunters had to apply force repeatedly to make stone tools, causing the material to fracture. They used blows

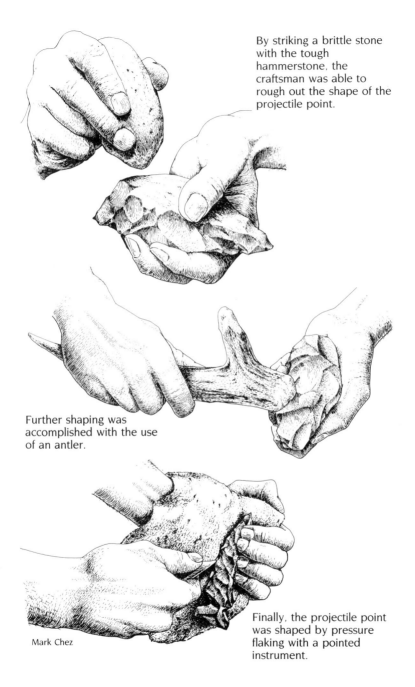

By striking a brittle stone with the tough hammerstone, the craftsman was able to rough out the shape of the projectile point.

Further shaping was accomplished with the use of an antler.

Finally, the projectile point was shaped by pressure flaking with a pointed instrument.

Mark Chez

Three steps in the reductive process of stone tool-making.

from a tougher hammerstone for this process, employing hammers of different weights and materials. Creating stone tools from the parent piece thus required the controlled application of force to create fracture lines. The use of such a deliberate technique helps differentiate human artifacts from natural stone.

One sign of stone tool use archaeologists look for is microscopic evidence of wear. The kind of damage along a tool edge, for example, differs according to the task it was used for and the type of material worked upon. Archaeologists, probably the world's only college-educated stone toolmakers, have conducted experiments to determine what kind of damage a stone tool sustains when used for butchering animals, whittling wood or for other tasks.

The level of craftsmanship in stone tools is also a subject of great interest to archaeologists. Some tools found in Alberta are made of materials from other areas, such as Knife River flint which comes from North Dakota. Other artifacts are so beautifully crafted that some wonder if they were meant for decoration, or for ceremonial purposes.

The way stone flakes are scattered over the landscape may also yield vital clues to past ways of life. The various stages of reduction required in stone tool manufacture generated a great deal of waste material, which sometimes allows archaeologists to learn about human movements on the landscape. Prehistoric people, for instance, may have preferred to use stone from a particular source. The litter from stone tool-making thus helps track prehistoric people's movements.

While stone tools were carried about and dispersed across the landscape, the waste flakes, or *debitage*, were immediately discarded.

"This allows us to make direct inferences about what took place," says Martin Magne, Head of the Research Section of the Archaeological Survey of Alberta. "Because tools were made, re-sharpened and modified at different rates and in different ways, depending on the tasks at hand, the debitage can be studied to understand these discrete events. With tools, what we have is a record of their last task, their final resting place, at the end of what may have been a complex use-span."

Archaeologists also learn about the stone tool users of the past from living stone tool-makers. Some Natives in British

Columbia and the Northwest Territories, for example, still manufacture chipped stone tools.

"By carrying out such "living archaeology" studies, archaeologists can witness both the aboriginal activities involving stone artifacts and the specific artifacts used," writes David Pokotylo in *Making and Using Stone Tools in British Columbia.* "They also have the opportunity to observe how human groups discard stone artifacts, a process that forms archaeological sites."

Stone arrangements are also important: the archaeological record of Alberta contains thousands of stone formations. They include cairns, medicine wheels, tipi rings and animal and human effigies. Although these stone formations will likely never reveal all their secrets, they do offer glimpses of prehistoric religious and social life.

Bones• Archaeologists have many reasons for studying animal bones or *faunal assemblages* at sites. The kinds of bone found are important when reconstructing the diet of prehistoric peoples. The presence of caribou, moose, hare, fish and bird bones shows a more generalized hunting economy and diet than does an abundance of bison bones. The same bones also give hints about cultural and circumstantial differences experienced by people long ago. Patterns of cut marks near joints betray different butchering strategies in the past, while the degree to which bone has been deliberately broken for marrow and grease provides clues about the dietary status of hunters and their families. The sex and age of animals taken can also help illustrate something of the hunting strategies used in the past.

In fleshing out their picture of the past, archaeologists often need to know in which season a site was occupied. Animal bones are particularly important to these studies. The presence of foetal remains at a kill suggests a spring hunt. Other clues about the season of death come from the annual growth rings in animal teeth, the characteristic sequence of eruption of teeth in younger animals and the wear patterns on teeth.

Finally, bone can be fractured, ground and polished. Prehistoric people fashioned bone into tools like needles, *awls* (larger than needles and used for punching), fleshing tools and scrapers. Such tools proved vital in tasks ranging from butchering and hide processing to the preparation of clothing and shelter.

Ceramics• Although prehistoric ceramics are rarely found in the mountains and boreal forest of Alberta, they are more common on the plains. Archaeologists refer to ceramics as an *additive technology*, because a potter starts with a lump of clay and then builds up the form. Clay is a more plastic medium than stone or bone, and therefore, is capable of expressing stylistic differences between groups more easily.

Rarely do whole prehistoric pots come to light in Alberta. Such pots are most frequently found by accident in lakes. Much more often, however, ceramics are presented to archaeologists as pieces from broken pots. Such pieces are called *potsherds*.

Much can be gleaned about a pot from studying its fragments. These can be classed as *rimsherds*, which are most often decorated with holes or patterns, sherds from the shoulder of the vessel, and sherds from the body of the vessel (the least distinctive). Archaeologists study these sherds to learn more about the manufacture of the pottery. They are interested in the source of clay used, for example, and the temper employed — the particles of sand or other material which prevents the pot from breaking when fired.

More exotic studies are also possible. Sometimes organic residues cling to potsherd surfaces. These residues can be analyzed to determine what the pot contained. Intriguingly, some prehistoric artisans left their fingerprints behind in the wet clay as they fashioned their pots, giving archaeologists a rare glimpse of individuals in prehistoric life.

All the prehistoric ceramics in Alberta were fired in hearths at relatively low temperatures. Such an environment created dull-coloured wares of brown and gray. Despite their lacklustre appearance, these ceramics can yield a rich store of information.

Palaeoenvironmental Studies

Palaeoenvironmental studies are often undertaken not so much by archaeologists as by specialists trained in geology, physical geography, soil sciences or botany. These studies make use of natural, organic materials in the archaeological record which can cast light on human activity. The soil

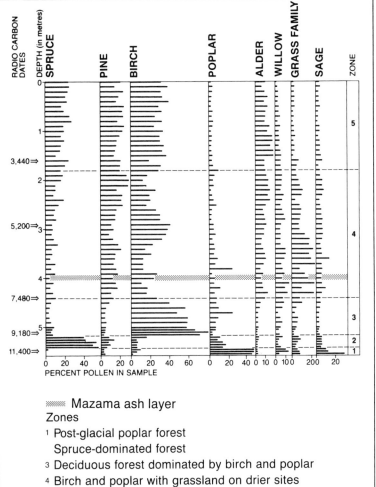

PERCENT POLLEN IN SAMPLE

▨▨▨ Mazama ash layer
Zones
1 Post-glacial poplar forest
  Spruce-dominated forest
3 Deciduous forest dominated by birch and poplar
4 Birch and poplar with grassland on drier sites
5 Less grassland, forest similar to modern boreal forest

Wendy Johnson/ASA

Pollen diagram from Lofty Lake, Alberta, shows the relative amounts of different pollen types identified in samples from a core of lake sediment, from the youngest sample (top) to the oldest (base). Each set of lines across the diagram represents a single sample. The sample at the 3440 year level contains ca. 25% spruce pollen, ca. 20% pine and birch pollen, less than 5% poplar pollen, ca. 10% alder pollen, and ca. 5% willow, grass and sage pollen, and was produced by vegetation similar to the modern southern boreal forest. The diagram is divided into five zones; the inferred vegetation is different in each zone, as shown by changes in the pollen percentages.

itself or plant remains help provide information about the kind of prehistoric environment humans lived in.

Pollen analysis is one tool employed in the study of prehistoric climates which often yields information important to archaeologists. The basis of this technique relies upon the fact that the material from which pollen is composed is not only distinctive between species, but is one of the most resistant compounds known. Under a microscope, scientists study pollen extracted from core samples of lake sediments, determining the presence of different species of plants by identification of the different grains.

Careful study of the frequency of different pollen types allows scientists to reconstruct changes in the vegetation of prehistoric landscapes and, from this, to infer climatic changes. We know from these studies that different locations in the province experienced tundra-like conditions near glaciers, while others were characterized by spruce forests, parkland and grasslands.

Another significant factor is the presence of prehistoric volcanic ash in southern Alberta. The ash most prevalent here originated from Mount Mazama (Crater Lake in Oregon). When it blew up about 6,700 years ago, the plume from the explosion spread across a large area of North America, including southern Alberta and Saskatchewan. The layer of ash, which can be several millimetres thick, is recognizable in some soil conditions and gives scientists another means of establishing dating. An earlier eruption of Mount St. Helen's, 3,400 years ago, also left traces of ash in Alberta.

If archaeologists are to increase our understanding of the people who lived in Alberta before the fur traders, they must then look to stones, bones, pollen and fragments of clay pots. But they must also have the vision to look beyond, to see what these mere objects reflect about the beliefs, values and ways of life of the first Albertans. Otherwise, as one Edmonton archaeologist recently reflected, we will end up only with a catalogue of dead buffalo.

Challenging as this search is, it has already yielded rich rewards. Alberta's archaeological record has already revealed a picture of a hunting society in southern Alberta whose complex strategies may have matched the ingenuity of the societies which built Stonehenge.

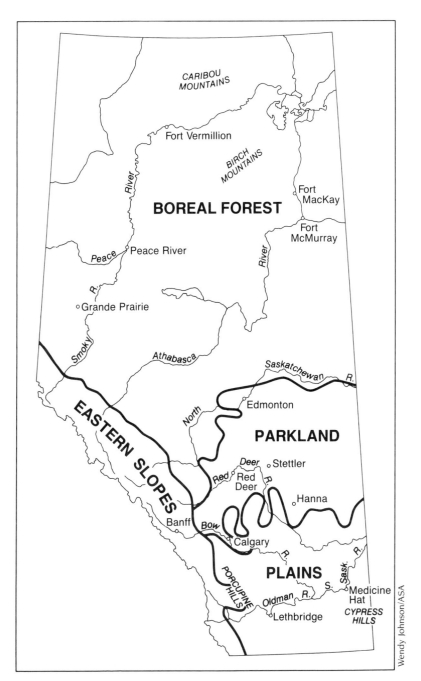

The major vegetation zones of Alberta.

The Window of Archaeology

The potential of archaeology to explain Alberta's past is especially exciting considering how young the discipline is in this province. Archaeology itself is barely 100-years-old. In Alberta, the discipline is far younger.

Beginning in the 1930s, a number of American archaeologists made periodic visits to Alberta, including Boyd Wettlaufer, who in 1949 began excavations at Head-Smashed-In. (The results of his investigations have never been published, a common enough occurrence in the earlier, more casual days of archaeology.) Many archaeologists, however, consider that archaeology did not begin in Alberta until 1955, when H. Marie Wormington, then with the Denver Museum of Natural History, began work under the direction of the Glenbow Foundation of Calgary. She was joined a few years later by Richard Forbis, often called the father of Alberta archaeology. Jointly they wrote *An Introduction to the Archaeology of Alberta, Canada*, the first book on Alberta archaeology and still an important reference.

The University of Calgary in 1964, became the first university in North America to offer a separate Department of Archaeolology. In 1973, the *Alberta Historical Resources Act* opened the way for the formation of the Archaeological Survey of Alberta, a branch of the Historical Resources Division of Alberta Culture. Its role is to investigate, protect and promote public appreciation of Alberta's archaeological heritage. Today, it employs twenty-two staff members, including ten professional archaeologists and researchers.

"My country has no history, only a past," wrote Canadian poet Alden Nowlan.

In Alberta, the past, as we have reconstructed it thus far, begins with a small band of hunters beside Vermilion Lakes in the Rocky Mountains.

Methy Portage: "A Most. . . Ravishing Prospect"

This precipice, which rises upwards of a thousand feet above the plain beneath it, commands a most extensive, romantic, and ravishing prospect. From thence the eye looks down on the course of the little river, by some called the Swan river, and by others, the Clear-Water and Pelican River, beautifully meandering for upwards of thirty miles. The valley, which is at once refreshed and adorned by it, is confined by two lofty ridges of equal height, displaying a most delightful intermixture of wood and lawn, and stretching on till the blue mist obscures the prospect. Some parts of the inclining heights are covered with stately forests, relieved by promontories of the finest verdure, where the elk and buffalo find pasture. These are contrasted by spots where fire has destroyed the woods, and left a dreary void behind it. Nor, when I beheld this wonderful display of uncultivated nature, was the moving scenery of human occupation wanting to complete the picture. From this elevated situation, I beheld my people, diminished, as it were, to half their size, employed in pitching their tents in a charming meadow, and among the canoes, which, being turned upon their sides, presented their reddened bottoms in contrast with the surrounding verdure. At the same time, the process of gumming them produced numerous small spires of smoke, which, as they rose, enlivened the scene, and at length blended with the larger columns that ascended from the fires where the suppers were preparing. It was in the month of September when I enjoyed the scene, of which I do not presume to give an adequate description; and as it was the rutting season of the elk, the whistling of that animal was heard in all the variety which the echoes could afford it.

— Alexander Mackenzie (1801), *Journal of Sir Alexander Mackenzie*

Don Inman

2

The Mystery of the Ice-Free Corridor

About 10,500 years ago, a band of hunters made their camp beside Vermilion Lakes in what is now Banff National Park. The group selected a campsite on the slopes of Mt. Edith, with stunning views across the large lakes to the strangely-shaped Mt. Rundle and the rounded ridge of Sulphur Mountain. Although their south-facing campsite stayed warmer and sunnier than the forested land on the other side of the lake, they nevertheless built the fires which gave today's archaeologists clues to their existence. They are the first-known Albertans. . . so far.

Those flames of long ago left tell-tale bits of charcoal, which archaeologists found strewn around an ancient *hearth*. Bone fragments, perhaps of bison, as well as a now-extinct species of bighorn sheep, were also scattered about the camp. The hunters left stone tools called *bifaces*, which they sharpened on both sides to a common edge and probably used as knives for butchering. Two post holes suggest the group may have erected a small shelter of wooden posts covered by skins.

No one knows how long the first-known Albertans stayed at Vermilion Lakes; the campsite may have been only a brief stopover for a few hunters. Yet, it remains a most significant signpost in Alberta's past.

The Vermilion Lakes hunters lived at the end of the Ice

(Opposite page) Vermilion Lakes hunters camped by Mt. Rundle.

Age, or *Pleistocene Epoch,* which began roughly two million years ago and ended 10,000 years ago. During this period of climatic oscillation, ice sheets periodically surged and advanced over the continent; at other times they greatly retreated or even disappeared. At their maximum, the sheets may have covered up to one-half of the continent's surface.

Ice sheets more than a kilometre thick once blanketed most of Canada. By 10,500 years ago, the time of the Vermilion Lakes hunters, the last ice sheets were rapidly receding from almost all of Alberta, exposing terrain that had been covered for hundreds of centuries.

Around the same time, the great Pleistocene mammals from south of the ice sheets began to vanish. Mammoths, camels, lion-like cats, horses, giant bison, caribou, elk, wolves, and sheep all then grazed or hunted in what is now Alberta. They mysteriously disappeared by 10,000 years ago. The reasons for this extinction are hotly debated, and both environmental change and human hunting are championed as the cause.

Many scientists doubt that the small population of human hunters likely present in North America at the time of extinction could have destroyed all the large mammals. Paul S. Martin of the University of Arizona, however, has postulated that if you started with a human population of approximately 100, and if each hunter killed only six mammoths a year, more than three million mammoths and mastodons would be wiped out within 500 years. Needless to say, his views are highly controversial.

Mammoths probably still inhabited Alberta at the time the Vermilion Lakes people made their campsite. No evidence has been uncovered, however, to indicate that these people were mammoth-hunters. No bones from the enormous, elephant-like mammals have been found at the site, although remains of mammoths which lived around the same time have been discovered in Bowness in Calgary.

Intriguing though the Vermilion Lakes site is, most archaeologists do not think the people who camped there represent the earliest occupants of the province.

"It is a very early site, but we can show that it is far too late to be evidence of the first entry of people into what is now this province," says ASA Director Jack Ives. "Vermilion Lakes is too late because, throughout adjacent parts of the U.S. and southern parts of Canada, prehistoric people were firmly established 11,500 years ago."

He calls Vermilion Lakes "simply the earliest site known. Yet it is in a location where we can predict evidence could be found for the first Albertans: the Ice-Free Corridor."

The tantalizing possibility of finding evidence of even earlier people has seized the imagination of many professionals and amateurs in the field, and doubtless represents the greatest challenge facing the discipline in this province.

Most agree that Banff is a good place to look. Archaeologist Darryl Fedje of Parks Canada, says the studies undertaken at Vermilion Lakes and other sites in the area are significant because they show that the environs of Banff National Park are far from marginal in terms of past cultural activity. "In fact, not only was this area used extensively throughout the past ten to twelve millenia, but the environment is of great benefit to archaeologists," he says, explaining that geological processes tended to bury and preserve archaeological sites in the Rockies, rather than to erode or destroy them, as so often happens on Alberta's Plains.

The best hope of archaeologists to find even earlier Albertans may thus lie in what may have been an ice-free corridor, thought to have existed along the Eastern Slopes of the Rocky Mountains in western Alberta. This ice-free area is believed to have occurred at the fluctuating juncture of the mountain (*Cordilleran*) and continental (*Laurentide*) ice masses, and is of major significance to a study of Alberta archaeology.

Many believe this ice-free corridor funnelled the first people into the heart of North America at various times during the last surge of glaciation, called the Wisconsinan. That period began about 75,000 years ago and lasted until about 10,000 years ago, about the time of the Vermilion Lakes campsite.

We know people lived south of the ice sheets, in what is now the United States, Mexico and South America, at a time when much of Canada, including Alberta, was still partly gripped in ice. But how did they get there?

The ice-free corridor theory offers an appealing explanation. It holds that the first prehistoric passage south from the region around the Bering Strait (Beringia) into the heart of North America opened between lobes of ice sheets along the Eastern Slopes of the Rocky Mountains. This provided a "highway" which stretched from the Yukon and Alaska into present-day Montana. The corridor, the theory goes, was open most of the time during the Late Wisconsinan. It extended 4,000 kilometres from the Richardson Mountains in the Yukon to the Lethbridge-Waterton Lakes region of southern Alberta, probably cutting through the present-day townsites of Edson, Nordegg, Rocky Mountain House and Calgary.

The answer to an enduring mystery — the peopling of the Americas — may be enshrouded within a mountainous ribbon of land which includes a lengthy portion in Alberta. A majority of archaeologists believe the interior of North America was first populated when ancestral Native Americans moved down that as yet elusive passage. The highly-advanced civilizations of ancient Peru and Mexico, the Pueblo dwellers of the American southwest and the mound-building societies of the southeastern U.S. all trace their origins to the people who made their way along the first great migration route, a passageway in which Alberta may have figured prominently.

There is another viewpoint. Some archaeologists believe the people who crossed what is now the Bering Strait into North America continued south by boat. According to this theory, some areas along the Pacific Coast were not totally glaciated during the Ice Age and the coastal waters would have been navigable.

Many archaeologists find the coastal migration theory to be unlikely. Such a journey would have required the development of sophisticated boat technology, and weapons suitable for maritime hunting and fishing. No evidence exists for these technological advances before 12,000 to 14,000 years ago. Moreover, the coast of British Columbia is like that of Norway: great stretches have only inhospitable cliffs, with the only points of access occurring at river mouths. During glacial periods, glaciers flowed down fjords and river valleys, and out into the sea. There, icebergs "calved" off. Rather than being safe havens, these areas were extremely dangerous. For these reasons, there is skepticism about a coastal route, although this alternative cannot be completely ruled out.

The ice-free corridor scenario, the one favoured by most archaeologists, means Alberta may hold the answer to the riddle of how the entire continent was populated. If even earlier Albertans are found than those at Vermilion Lakes, their campsites may offer evidence of the corridor's use as a migration route south.

Vermilion Lakes: Clovis?

Finding signs of human habitation in Alberta before the Vermilion Lakes hunters could solve a mystery that has puzzled generations since Christopher Columbus first landed in the Bahamas in 1492. As late as 1930, many scientists still rejected the idea that people had been in the Americas for more than about 3,000 years. There had once been suggestions that Indians came from India; others considered them descendants of the Lost Tribes of Israel.

Then, in 1926, J. D. Figgins discovered stone projectile points in undisputed association with extinct forms of bison at Folsom, New Mexico. This find proved that prehistoric Natives had been present in North America late in the Pleistocene. By 1932, new finds came to light at Clovis, New Mexico, where archaeologists discovered the bones of butchered mammoths, along with chipped stone spearheads. These remains are now known to be 11,500 years of age; they predate the Folsom finds.

In their own way, these *Clovis* points are almost as distinctive as any slug fired from the rifled barrel of a .45 automatic. They feature points with a specially thinned base and a spear tip defined as *lanceolate* — long, thin and tapering at one or both ends. Flakes of stone were chipped vertically to create a *flute* or groove, and the fluted area was then attached to a spear shaft.

Between 11,500 and 11,000 years ago, the people who made these or similar points swept through a continent which seems to have been otherwise unoccupied. Fluted points are known from all over the United States and southern Canada, and surface finds have been made in Alberta. Fluted points also occur in Central America, and fluted fishtail points with reasonably reliable equivalent dates have been found as far south as Tierra del Fuego.

These Clovis hunters preyed on the giant Ice Age mammals,

particularly the *mammoth*, with such skill that some scientists claim they were responsible for the sudden disappearance of the giant elephants between 12,000 and 10,000 years ago. A well-known American Plains archaeologist, George Frison, has actually shown through experiments with elephants being culled from herds in Africa, that replicated Clovis points can inflict fatal wounds on large mammals. Although this is not the kind of archaeological research most would volunteer for, it has helped to verify the skills of the Clovis hunters.

Understanding the extremely rapid, widespread distribution of fluted points and their equivalents is vital to answering the crucial question of how the continent was first peopled. Archaeologists want to know whether the continent was populated quickly by Clovis hunters, or whether the process occurred more gradually, perhaps between 10,500 and 15,000 years ago.

(Left) Clovis
Approximately
11,000-10,500 years ago
Folsom
Approximately
11,000-11,500 years ago

Two examples of projectile points (shown actual size) of the Early Prehistoric Period.

Danek Mozdzenski

38

Either the use of Clovis points spread from North America to Chile in about 1,000 years, or an earlier influx occurred. Scientists do not know if the people who made Clovis points were the first humans to venture south of the ice sheets, but the Clovis appearance of 11,500 years ago remains the earliest undisputed date for human occupation that far south.

Did "pre-Clovis" people, as archaeologists refer to them, journey south of the ice? If they did, can their traces be found in the ice-free corridor, which seems the most likely place? These are the vital questions.

No one can be certain where Clovis technology originated or what it represents. The few fluted point finds in Alaska and the Yukon all seem too recent to be ancestral. The presence of Clovis points across North America may signify a physical influx of people carrying a distinctive lifestyle and tool kit. It could also represent the adoption of a distinctive lifestyle and tool kit by people already present 11,500 years ago. Some archaeologists, as discussed in Chapter 1, are quick to equate points with people; others believe the dynamics behind style changes may be far more elusive.

Although the answers to the preceding questions are far from clear, archaeologists believe they may yet solve them by looking back to the dimly-seen figures who first tiptoed onto the New World.

A Land of Steppe-Tundra and Woolly Mammoth

Today, you can stand on the coastal tundra of Alaska and look across the Bering Strait to eastern Siberia — less than 100 kilometres separate the New World from the Old. Scientists agree that the first migrations to this continent likely took place across a land bridge at this point which once connected North America with Asia.

The land connection was not constant. As Ice Age glaciers formed, they locked in great quantities of water. This caused world ocean levels to drop by as much as 100 metres during colder periods, thus exposing a land bridge for sporadic groups of hunters to cross.

Some scientists believe the land connection held roughly from about 70,000 to 50,000 years ago and again from about 25,000 to 14,000 years ago, while glaciation was occurring in North America. But no one can say when people first entered North America or what their origins were. One theory is that these hunters originated by advancing around the Pacific Rim from East Asia; another is that they migrated across Siberia.

Beringia is the name given to the land mass (named after and including the Bering Strait) which now encompasses parts of eastern Russia, Alaska and the interior Yukon. A diverse environment including mountains, plateaus and rivers, Beringia is of great interest to archaeologists because it formed the most likely pathway for humans to enter North America.

What kind of landscape did the early hunters find in Beringia? The subject is intensely debated. Some scientists believe the kinds of animals found there were so varied and abundant that the best modern-day equivalent is found on the African savannahs. They refer to such a landscape as a "mammoth steppe" or "steppe-tundra." (Tundra refers to the vast, treeless terrain of the Arctic regions of North America, Europe and Asia, while steppe is the term applied to the grasslands of Eurasia, which are quite similar to the grasslands of North America.)

Other scientists believe that the physical evidence for steppe-tundra is lacking, and hold instead that only a few animals may have inhabited Beringia. In part, they base these views on pollen analysis, which indicates the vegetation may have resembled tundra more than steppe. This less productive vegetation would not have been able to support large numbers of different animals. The question remains unresolved and is referred to as "the productivity paradox."

Charles Schweger, a palaeoecologist with the Department of Anthropology at the University of Alberta, gives the following view of the Beringian landscape:

> During the Wisconsinan, valleys of Eastern Beringia would have represented a relatively favorable environment. Valley-bottom vegetation assured abundant fodder, and valleys provided shelter for animals, which like those of today must have had to endure long and cold winters.

Schweger warns, however, that any attempt to reconstruct Ice Age vegetation patterns exclusively on the basis of modern vegetation patterns, which exist without the influence of the extinct Pleistocene mammals, "may be naive."

Fortunately, more is known about the animal life of Pleistocene Beringia than of its vegetation. The new grazing grounds appear to have attracted one of the most exotic menageries imaginable. Huge woolly mammoths, whose closest relatives are the modern Asian elephant, roamed this strange world. So did sabre-toothed cats the size of lions, giant bison with flaring horns, large wolves, hyenas, caribou and musk ox, camels, saiga antelope, wild asses, and mastodons. In other words, an animal kingdom of spectacular diversity may have stretched from Europe to the Yukon. This assortment of wildlife included animals we see today only in the grasslands or

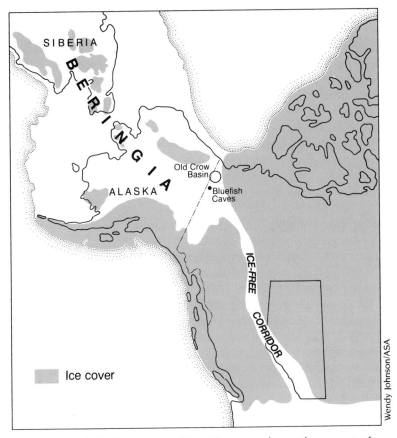

Beringia and the ice-free corridor. The map shows the extent of Beringia in northern North America approximately 18,000 years ago. Also shown is the location and path of the ice-free corridor thought to exist about 14,000 to 12,000 years ago.

only on the tundra. Some archaeologists believe this animal community may well have provided the incentive to early human hunters to adapt to extreme northern environments, and the resulting Arctic adaptation brought people to Beringia, to Alberta and ultimately to the rest of the Americas.

People Arrive in North America

These initial human players on a new continent's stage, then, were probably not explorers in quest of a new land. Their goal was not to escape one continent for another; they were simply hunters pursuing game into another region.

Theoretically, people might have entered the Americas 80,000 to 120,000 years ago. We know the Stone Age residents of Europe, Neanderthal men and women, had at least begun to make seasonal use of open, cold environments. But if humans were in the Americas that long ago, no incontrovertible evidence of their passing has been found.

The most widely-accepted theory is that people reached eastern Beringia sometime during the most recent exposure of the Bering Shelf (the land bridge), between about 25,000 and 14,000 years ago. The earliest evidence from an archaeological site places the first humans in North America in the Yukon roughly 16,000 to 18,000 years ago.

Bone and stone artifacts dating back that far have been discovered in the Bluefish Caves, three small caves in the Keele range on the Canadian side of the Alaska-Yukon border. This site, situated just north of the ice-free corridor, places people in a position to enter interior North America 4,000 years before Clovis.

No confirmed artifacts older than those at Bluefish Caves have been reliably dated. Across the land bridge, however, parts of eastern Siberia (Western Beringia) may have been occupied for more than 30,000 years. A question haunting modern archaeology is whether people entered this continent thousands of years, even tens of thousands of years, before Bluefish.

Life in Beringia and Beyond

Archaeologists face formidable problems in attempting to illuminate our knowledge of the first North Americans. The Bering land bridge itself, after all, has lain underwater for

12,000 years. The large-scale development and greater number of people which have unearthed so many archaeological sites in the rest of the continent are not characteristic of the Arctic. Moreover, the few stone and bone tools that appear in the archaeological record tell us little about the early peoples' way of life, beyond hunting. We know nothing of their beliefs, values and aspirations — or even of their dwellings or dress.

Archaeologists can, however, make some inferences based on their understanding of other prehistoric people who lived in Europe. Outside North America, archaeologists have found signs of successful cold-weather adaptations going as far back as 27,000 years. One fascinating way to begin exploring the lifestyle of the first Beringian hunters is to travel back to Europe in the time between 50,000 and 100,000 years ago . . .

People of the Central Russian Plain

During that little-known period, our own species, *Homo sapiens*, had not yet appeared in Europe. The continent was instead inhabited by our close evolutionary relative, Neanderthal man (*Homo sapiens neanderthalensis*), who made some use of northern environments and is known to have had camps further north than the 49th parallel, in tundra-like conditions.

By 34,000 years ago, our own, fully modern human species had appeared in Europe. To the north and east lay a game-rich steppe-tundra, which may have been unhunted. By between 30,000 and 27,000 years ago, sophisticated hunters seem to have begun expanding from Czechoslovakia, across European Russia and towards Siberia. Archaeologists know these people had solved certain cold-climate problems. The discovery of awls and needles, for instance, shows they knew how to make effective Arctic garments. Garments like parkas are also evident on sculpted figurines from this time period.

More may be learned about their adaptations from recent discoveries in the heart of the Ukraine. On the Russian Plain near present-day Kiev, archaeologists like Olga Soffer of the University of Illinois have discovered unmistakable signs of a prehistoric society which flourished despite the cold temperatures of the last glacial period. Archaeologists have identified two periods of occupation, between 26,000 and 20,000 years, and between 18,000 and 12,000 years.

Game on the Russian grasslands resembled Beringia's. Great herds of mammoth, bison, reindeer and horses wandered, along with lion-like cats, giant bears and wolves. The choice trophy was mammoth. Indeed, a single mammoth yielded so much meat that these hunters invented cold storage systems to prevent spoilage. They also used mammoth bone and ivory to make weapons and tools.

These people built groups of remarkable dwellings, usually in sheltered areas used as winter base camps. Soffer estimates many of the dwellings might have taken eighteen days to erect with a construction crew of ten. Some were framed entirely of mammoth leg bones, others of jawbones. Especially in the later period, larger houses were ringed by a series of hearths, probably used by families.

The artistry which went into their design is particularly apparent at a site called Mezhirich. At one dwelling, for instance, two rows of jawbones were stacked chin down, followed by one row placed chin up. Other rows follow an alternating pattern composed of shoulderblades and skulls.

The mammoth-hunters lived around the same time as gifted sculptors and engravers in the Dordogne region of France. They too were exquisite craftsmen. They fashioned chubby Venus-like figurines of sandstone, ivory and fired clays; they worked amber and fossil marine shells into fine jewelry.

Archaeologists believe these hunters participated in long-distance trading networks. Neither amber nor marine shells occur naturally on the Russian Plains — the closest amber deposits are 300 kilometres distant and the closest marine shell deposits 700 kilometres.

From the way people were buried in this region, archaeologists also detect traces of highly-developed social and political organization. Objects made from rare and valuable materials usually indicate status among hunting peoples. When they are found at burial sites, archaeologists call them *grave goods*. On the Russian Plain, some individuals were buried with rich grave goods composed of thousands of bone or ivory beads, pendants, needles and other tools.

Where does the preceding time trek back to Europe lead in trying to cast light on the Beringian hunters? Clearly, no one is suggesting this Central Plain society formed the population from which Native North Americans (and hence Albertan Natives) came. That view is too simplistic. The example, however, illustrates that an early, highly-successful society of hunters lived far beyond a basic level of survival in an environment similar to Beringia's.

Two Technological Traditions in Eastern Siberia and Beringia?

Archaeologists trying to trace the origins of the first North Americans not only look for clues in the cold-weather adaptations of eastern Siberia, but also to resemblances found there with the stone tool industries of prehistoric North America. The people of the Dyuktai culture of eastern Siberia hunted and trapped the same animals as the Beringians 18,000 to 20,000 years ago. These people made use of stone technology which included similar tools, including bifacial projectile points. They also employed small wedge-shaped *cores* made out of stone, from which *microblades* were fashioned.

Archaeologists find similar wedge-shaped microcores and microblades in the Alaska Region by 10,500 to 11,000 years ago. Many scientists see affinities between them and earlier Dyuktai materials.

Yet another tradition of stone tool-making is found in eastern Siberia, one which resembles those of the Central Plains more than Dyuktai. The remains of human habitation occurring between 20,000 to 22,000 years ago have been found at sites such as Mal'ta and Buret on the upper Angara River, and Afontova Gora on the Yenisei River. These people made stone tools including bifaces, sidescrapers and flake projectile points. No signs of microcore and microblade industry appear at any of these sites.

There are, however, many indications of advanced societies. At Mal'ta and Buret, for example, people lived in dwellings lined with stone slabs or mammoth bones. They appear, from the presence of cache pits, to have stored food and used red ochre in burials, undoubtedly for ceremonial purposes.

From these sites, archaeologists conclude there were at least two technological traditions in eastern Siberia, and probably on the Bering platform itself, between 12,000 and 20,000 years ago.

Vance Haynes of the University of Arizona points out that Clovis has intriguing similarities with the Mal'ta-Afontova sites. He sees similarities in the bifacial projectile points; the bevelled-base cylindrical bone points and foreshafts; the use of red ochre with grave goods; and, the presence of large blades from prismatic cores. He points out that microcores and microblades are not known from any Clovis sites.

Another Clue in Biology

Scientists look to another kind of evidence besides archaeology for the origin of New World Native populations. When physical anthropologists study the human biology of aboriginal populations in the Americas, their findings invariably lead them to look to northeast Asia for the origins of these peoples. They find great similarities in general traits, such as the dominance of straight, black hair, a broad facial structure and high cheek bones.

There are also more specific points of comparison, such as tooth shape. New World Natives have a dental pattern referred to as *sinodonty* (from the root words for China and for teeth). The most important distinguishing feature of this pattern is the persistent presence of shovel-shaped incisors, rather than the blade-like incisors of other populations. Blood group systems, including the A-B-O system familiar to us from blood bank donations, also show distinctive similarities with northeast Asia.

Although the subject of considerable debate among scientists, a current theory relies upon evidence of this sort to suggest that three waves of migration took place into North America. The first wave is now represented by all Indians of the Americas who live from southern North America to South America. The second wave was comprised of peoples who came to live in coastal British Columbia and the northwest interior of North America. Ancestors of Inuit and Aleuts — the people now found from coastal and interior Alaska, across the Canadian north and in Greenland — comprised the final wave.

Whether or not such a scenario is realistic, virtually all physical anthropologists see northeastern Asia, including eastern Siberia and northern China, as the point of origin for North and South American Indians.

The Paleo-Indian World

The first people to enter North America, regardless of their cultural origins, probably maintained social and trade links with Asia as long as a land bridge existed between the two continents.

They must have attained a high degree of technological and cultural sophistication. Life in those latitudes required warm, secure dwellings, clothing tailored to keep out the cold, reliable hunting methods and the control of fire.

"Some writers have suggested that the ancient colonization of Beringia represented a technological achievement equivalent to the penetration of such environments as Antarctica, the deep sea and the moon," notes archaeologist Richard Morlan of the Archaeological Survey of Canada, in *The Canadian Encyclopedia*.

Archaeologists believe those first hunters carried tools of bone, stone and ivory. They must have had knives for cutting, choppers for butchering and scrapers for hide preparation. They probably carried thrusting spears with large stone and bone points.

On the open landscape, they probably used animal dung to fuel their fires. They wore clothing made of skins and fur, sewn with bone or ivory awls. They likely framed their dwellings with animal bones and covered them with hides. They may have brought with them domesticated dogs, their only beast of burden.

Hunting and Gathering

The Beringian hunters brought with them hunting and gathering — perhaps humanity's oldest ways of life.

No one is certain when humans began to live by hunting animals and gathering wild plants. A still-earlier way of life may have been scavenging from the kills of wild predators. What we do know is that by 30,000 to 40,000 years ago, hunters and gatherers around the globe had perfected the techniques of big-game hunting and harvesting wild fruits and seeds. It was an adaptation that made survival possible in every environment and on every continent except Antarctica.

Traditionally, hunters and gatherers were highly mobile, roaming across the land in small bands as game and plant populations fluctuated from region to region. There are some exceptions, although not in Alberta. Some hunters and gatherers, including those on the West Coast of British Columbia, organized themselves into tribal societies and chiefdoms and lived in permanent or semi-permanent settlements. This only occurred where an abundance of resources, such as fish or edible plants, permitted.

In general, the closer hunters and gatherers lived to the tropics, the more they relied on gathering plants for food. In the cooler zones of Europe and North America, big-game hunting dominated.

The Move South: Through the Ice-Free Corridor?

The connection between Asia and North America was severed for the last time about 14,000 years ago, when global temperatures increased and rising ocean levels flooded much of Beringia. But even before the land bridge closed, the people of eastern Beringia had started their movement southwards, perhaps following the ice-free corridor. Because of the ice, the remainder of the terrain south of Beringia would have been highly inhospitable.

During the Late Wisconsinan, the massive Laurentide ice sheet, originating in the Hudson Bay region, blanketed most of Canada as far west as the Eastern Slopes of the Rockies. A second ice mass, the Cordilleran, consisted of a series of developing ice-caps which likely came together in some areas. Along the Eastern Slopes, a series of ice tongues probably spilled out of major valleys, with large ice-free areas in between. Although the margins of both ice sheets advanced and retreated at various times, the fluctuations of the Laurentide and Cordilleran ice masses likely did not occur at the same time.

One problem for scientists trying to track these fluctuations is that glacial advances and retreats have occurred many times in the last two million years. Each advance can obliterate evidence of earlier advances. Sometimes, it is believed the two sheets united and flowed southward together, as demonstrated by the Foothills Erratics Train. This series of large boulders called *erratics* (the most famous is the "Big Rock" at Okotoks), stretches from the Athabasca Valley to Montana. The rocks were carried by Cordilleran ice flowing down the Athabasca Valley, which met with Laurentide ice and was deflected towards the southeast.

Nat Rutter, chairman of the Geology Department at the University of Alberta, has argued that ice-free conditions in the corridor area were probably the rule, rather than the exception, during Wisconsinan time, that is, during the last 75,000 years.

Rutter, in a paper entitled "Pleistocene History of the Western Canadian Ice-Free Corridor," notes little is known about conditions in the corridor area during the Early Wisconsinan, and no glacial activity has been detected during the Middle Wisconsinan. He is far more definite about glacial activity during Late Wisconsinan time, beginning about 25,000 years ago and ending about 10,000 years ago.

"During Late Wisconsinan time, Laurentide glaciers advanced as far west as Lethbridge, Calgary, and Edson in southern Alberta, whereas Cordilleran glaciers terminated near the mountain front or within the major valleys," he says. "Therefore, an ice-free corridor was present from about the International Boundary to the Jasper-Hinton area."

In the Yukon Territory and the Northwest Territories, Rutter says, continental Laurentide glaciers extended into the Mackenzie and Richardson mountains, "but Cordilleran ice did not advance far down the mountain valleys, resulting in an ice-free corridor in this region."

The ramifications for Albertans are fascinating, and hotly debated. If an ice-corridor existed through this part of the province for most of the Late Wisconsinan, it could have been a passageway for Beringian hunters making their way south.

Or could it have been? If prehistoric people passed through this corridor, they probably did not find it hospitable. Although only small tongues of ice may have protruded into the corridor itself, the presence of large amounts of ice on either side would obviously have affected the climate in many ways, none of them pleasant. Strong, chill winds probably blew down from the ice sheets. Glacial lakes, formed by meltwater, would have further contributed to the dank, chill environment. Vegetation was likely sparse, perhaps resembling that of parts of Beringia, with grasses, sedge and sage dominating.

The possibilities tempt the imagination, yet scientists caution that much more research is needed to test the ice-free corridor theory.

Despite uncertainty over the first appearance of humans in the corridor area, the archaeological value of the region is now undisputed. Eastern Slopes archaeologist Brian Ronaghan of the ASA says the richness and diversity of the archaeological record of the Eastern Slopes recovered to date "demonstrates that the area later functioned as a major prehistoric exploitation zone rather than simply a travel corridor between the plains and plateau culture areas."

The Search Today

In years to come, new evidence and new arguments will certainly be found to help explain how the first people reached the interior of North America. In Alberta, hopes are pinned on the results of a five-year research effort, initiated by the ASA in the summer of 1987. The ASA will search for traces of the first people who lived in this province, the hunters who may predate the Vermilion Lakes group and represent the first influx of humans into the heart of the continent.

Research teams will survey the Eastern Slopes of the Rockies, searching out caves west of Grande Prairie and analyzing pollen samples, among other projects. Their ambitious goals are not only to learn if an ice-free corridor existed and if humans could have lived in such an environment before 11,500 years ago, but to try to track down actual campsites, an exciting prospect indeed.

Although the quest may seem impossible to many, archaeologists will apply their combined knowledge of past geological, environmental and cultural conditions to search those areas which appear to be the most likely candidates for prehistoric habitation. Jack Ives admits that the risks are great of not finding anything in this earliest time range. But he believes Alberta has a responsibility to the rest of the world to at least try.

Even if systematic searching by the ASA proves fruitless, Ives says the very fact it has been carried out will stand as a significant contribution to worldwide archaeology, which still heatedly debates the way in which prehistoric people migrated into the Western hemisphere.

If Alberta research can find traces of pre-Clovis hunters (which would suggest that North America was populated over a long period of perhaps 10,000 to 15,000 years, instead of a short 500-year Clovis explosion) it would be an event of electrifying international importance.

Says Ives: "There's no question in my mind we'll find something worthwhile, even if the important sites discovered come from later time periods."

The Ice Retreats

The great ice sheets which had long frozen the province into an icy tomb vanished relatively quickly between 13,000 and 10,000 years ago. The newly-exposed landscape was occupied first by a tundra-like vegetation, which probably contained few trees, except for poplar. Spruce-dominated forests then replaced the landscape over much of the province. In southern Alberta, prairie vegetation likely replaced the forest sometime between about 10,000 and 9,000 years ago.

"When deglaciation finally occurred in Alberta, the newly-exposed terrain wouldn't have been clothed immediately in the same vegetation that grows in the area today," explains Alwynne Beaudoin, palaeoenvironmental research officer with the ASA. "It took time for plants to colonise the landscape, for plants to migrate into recently-deglaciated areas, and for soils to develop."

Two dominant environments emerged as the ice receded, the boreal forest and the plains, and two quite different ways of life developed within them. Each approach, in its own way, proved equally successful.

The Mystery of the Giant Mammals

The woman visitor couldn't wait to share what she had found while walking in the Whitemud Creek area near Edmonton.

"She came up with a piece of mastodon tooth," recalls Jim Burns, curator of Quaternary Palaeontology at the Provincial Museum of Alberta. "It was rather exciting. There are only four specimens of mastodons in Alberta."

Mastodons are perhaps the most exotic of the rich menagerie of giant Ice Age mammals (Pleistocene megafauna) which once inhabited Alberta, but they are far from being the only ones. From the Medicine Hat area a few remains of a sabre-toothed cat have been found; in Peace River Country the molar of a mammoth, a rare item indeed, has been discovered. Evidence of prehistoric camels has been found in Calgary, and Cochrane and Medicine Hat.

Alberta was also once inhabited by lions, slightly larger than the African type, as well as ground sloths and several kinds of musk-oxen. No evidence has yet appeared of the presence of short-faced bears, believed comparable in size to Alaska's Kodiaks, but such evidence has been found in Saskatchewan. Nor is there any sign of giant beaver in Alberta, "but we're still looking," says Burns.

The bison is the most abundant of Ice Age mammals found in this province. Bones of bison from 5,000 to 6,000 years ago have even been found behind the Macdonald Hotel in downtown Edmonton. Says Burns: "We're up to our knees in bison."

Rarely are whole skeletons found. Usually scientists find bits of bone -- often teeth, which preserve well. Gravel pits, the remains of old rivers which the animals presumably drank from, are particularly rich sources of prehistoric mammal bones.

Scientists are uncertain why Pleistocene mammals grew so large. A common theory holds that animals which live farther north or at higher altitudes will grow bigger than their close relatives because they

52

Sabre-Tooth Cat

Camel

Bison

Mastodon

Sloth

Small horse

Ewa Pluciennik

Exotic bestiary of the Ice Age (Pleistocene megafauna).

face colder conditions. The physiological basis for this belief is that as animals triple their body weight they only double their surface area, so that the amount of heat loss they suffer is generally lower than that of smaller animals. The theory, however, is not accepted by all.

A greater puzzle is why these giant Ice Age mammals disappeared from North America between 9,000 and 12,000 years ago. There is certainly no lack of theories. One patient scientist ascertained that up to 1970, eighty-five hypotheses existed to explain Ice Age extinctions!

"Despite many attempts to clarify it, the cause of extinction has proved elusive to those geologists and biologists most familiar with the evidence," states Paul S. Martin in *Pleistocene Extinctions, The Search for a Cause*.

Some scientists point to climatic change, although that would conceivably imply a hitherto-unknown magnitude of change. Others believe intensified competition, due to alterations in range conditions, may have spelled the end to the giant beasts. Still others say the cause was over-hunting by humans, although it now seems doubtful if a single factor could explain such a profound event as extinction.

The alertness of highway crews, and others whose work involves deep excavation of Alberta soils, can greatly help to unearth more information about Alberta's Ice Age mammalian legacy.

The Truth Behind the Taber Child

Difficulties in dating artifacts present archaeology with one of its most formidable challenges in the search for early North Americans.

In 1966, archaeologists excavating in the Old Crow area of the northern Yukon discovered a fleshing tool fashioned out of caribou bone, which radiocarbon dating showed to be 27,000-years-old. This find galvanized new research for years. But recently, using more modern dating methods, scientists discovered the tool was less than 2,000-years-old.

Alberta has its own version of Old Crow. In 1961, geologists discovered a few bones of a young child along the Oldman River near Taber, in southern Alberta. The location of the bones suggested that they were very old, belonging to a child who perhaps lived 18,000 years ago.

Interest peaked among both the public and the scientific community, for the find suggested that humans were present in the New World *before* the end of the last Ice Age. Scientists from the National Museum of Man, the Canadian Conservation Institute and the Atomic Energy of Canada began to investigate the find.

What they found, however, did not live up to the expectations of many. Alberta archaeologists excavated the site and discovered recent mud-flow channels were present, indicating the bones could have come from a recent deposit. Analysis of the soil clinging to the bones also suggested they were deposited recently. Next, a chemical comparison of the protein content of the bones with both modern and Ice Age bone specimens, indicated a greater similarity to the more recent specimens. Finally, using a new accelerator dating technique, the bones of the Taber Child were revealed to be only about 3,500-years-old.

Archaeologists caution that we should not feel disappointed the Taber Child did not prove to be as ancient as once thought. They say the Taber Child stands today as an example of what can be accomplished by Canadian scientists using a multidisciplinary approach and the most modern techniques.

Armin Dyck excavating at Head-Smashed-In.

3

Buffalo-Hunting
on Alberta's Plains

 Amateur archaeologist Armin Dyck squinted at the long sandy ridge which snaked through an otherwise flat field near a friend's ranch. The wind raked his face. Brown grasslands roll to the horizon in that part of southern Alberta, about eighty kilometres southeast of Lethbridge. Dyck could see three buttes of the Sweetgrass Hills rising sixty kilometres to the south in Montana. Other than a ranch building or two, there was little else to look at.

A small, isolated and windy ridge sounds an unlikely destination for any living creature except a prairie gopher. Dyck saw it differently. He had, after all, found his first arrowhead, "a side-notched point," along the Oldman River when he was six-years-old.

Finding a few hours to spare that spring day in 1963, Dyck saddled a horse and headed toward the ridge which he had already scouted the year before.

"It looked like there might have been water in it at some time, and I thought: 'Where there's water, there's animals, and when there's animals, there's people,'" recalls Dyck, who now lives in Coaldale, Alberta.

His archaeological intuition was clicking like a geiger counter. The owner of the land, Frank Fletcher of Purple Springs, had recently heard tales of an old spring in the area below the ridge. Acting on the tip, the rancher used heavy equipment to excavate a water hole for his livestock.

When Dyck reached the dugout, he immediately realized the rancher had uncovered much more than water. Fragments of bone were spewed on the earth all around the fresh water hole.

He knew the bones were heavily mineralized from their deep bluish-black colour. They were obviously from buffalo much larger than today's. More examination revealed five or six spear tips among the bones. Dyck knew by their shape they must be 8,000 to 9,000-years-old.

"Bingo! I could see all these bone fragments," says Dyck. "I knew I was inches away from having some sort of attack, I was so excited."

Dyck jumped on his horse, galloped back to the ranch and, without saying a word to anyone about his find, caught the bus to Calgary that night.

The next day he presented the projectile points to archaeologist Richard Forbis, then of the Glenbow Foundation in Calgary. He confirmed what Dyck had suspected: this was the first buried archaeological site of Paleo-Indians so far discovered in Alberta, and an amateur had stumbled onto it.

A Prehistoric Marsh Speaks

The Fletcher site, as it came to be called after the name of the property owner, is a milestone in the annals of Alberta archaeology. Here is our best glimpse at the first well-established occupants of Alberta, the late *Paleo-Indians*.

We know the Fletcher hunters were glorious craftsmen in that they left distinctive traces — big, stemmed spear points of stone, in styles called *Alberta* and *Scottsbluff.*

Archaeologists also unearthed hammerstones for bone-breaking and stone knives (bifaces) flaked on both sides. The bison bones could not be accurately dated because of contamination from ground water. From the artifacts though, the site is believed to date to about 9,000 years ago.

What happened by the marsh so long ago?

"Most likely the Paleo-Indians ambushed a herd which had come to water at the slough," says Plains archaeologist Rod Vickers of the ASA. "I expect this might have been a communal *surround.*"

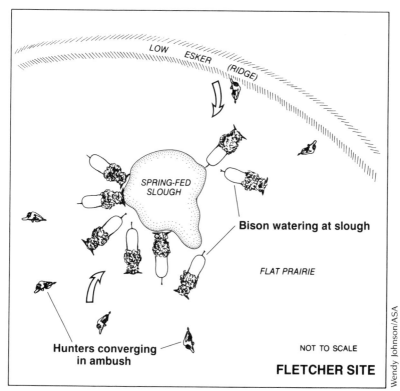

Wendy Johnson/ASA

Reconstruction of the bison kill at the Fletcher site. Hunters likely ambushed a small herd of bison watering at a small slough.

British-born explorer Henry Kelsey provided the first recorded description of a buffalo surround. His account, contained in *The Kelsey Papers*, stems from his encounters with Indians of the Northern Plains in 1691:

> This instant ye Indians going a hunting Kill'd/great store of Buffillo Now ye manner of their hunting/these Beast on ye Barren ground is when they see a great /parcel of them together they surround them with men whc done/they gather themselves into a smaller Compass Keeping/ye Beast still in ye middle & so shooting ym till they/break out at some place or other & so gett away from/ym.

By ambushing the bison in the marsh, the hunters could gain an important advantage: the unsuspecting animals could not escape as speedily from the soft ground as they could on the hard-packed prairie. (The Paleo-Indians hunted on foot — the horse became extinct in North America at the end of

the Ice Age. According to historic records, the horse was reintroduced by Spanish conquistador Hernando Cortez in 1519, but it did not again appear in Alberta until roughly A.D. 1730.)

Cooperating to Catch Buffalo

Most archaeologists conclude that by 9,000 years ago, people who specialized in communal hunting of bison roamed Alberta's Southern Plains.

The hunters' origins are unclear. The Alberta Plains, though, form a pocket easily open to influence from the south,

(Above left) Alberta
Approximately 9,500-8,900 years ago
(Above right) Scottsbluff
Approximately 9,000-8,300 years ago
(Right) Eden
Approximately 9,000-8,300 years ago

Three examples of projectile points (shown actual size) of the Early Prehistoric Period which make up the Cody Complex.

Danek Mozdzenski

60

southwest and east. Travel and contact with the west is blocked by mountains and the north was sparsely populated through the boreal forest.

To the south, the Northern Plains continued through what is now Montana, North and South Dakota, Wyoming and Nebraska and to the east into southern Saskatchewan and Manitoba. Traces of Paleo-Indian hunters have been found throughout this huge expanse dated between 11,500 and 7,500 years ago — a span archaeologists call the Early Prehistoric Period.

The new Alberta and Scottsbluff spear tips which the Fletcher hunters carried are known for their exquisitely-fashioned square and broad bases and precision-flaked blades. Hunters chipped them out of exceptionally good quality stone.

Archaeologists lump these and similar spear tips under the umbrella term *Cody Complex*. (The name stems from a 9,000-year-old Paleo-Indian site found in Cody, Wyoming.) A complex describes the archaeological remains of people living at the same time with similar technologies and ways of life.

Cody Complex traces have largely evaded the searching whiskbrooms and trowels of Alberta archaeologists. Part of the reason may be that the Paleo-Indians occupied a land still heaving in transition.

A period of warming began around 12,000 years ago. To the north and east, the great glacial lakes left by the Ice Age were quickly retreating. These included Glacial Lake Edmonton, which stretched from where the city now stands to Lake Wabamun, and Glacial Lake Agassiz, a huge inland sea covering one-third of the provinces of Manitoba and Saskatchewan.

The spruce forest that once stretched south beyond Lethbridge probably died out by 10,500 years ago, replaced by grasslands which extended as far north as the North Saskatchewan River and as far west as the Rockies. (That, at least, is the best guess of palaeoenvironmentalists who study past climates. They cannot be certain because lake and pond sediments for pollen analysis are often absent on the plains. See Chapter 2.)

After about 6,000 years ago, glacial till (deposits of loose rocks left behind by the Ice Age) eroded down and covered the old land surface so thoroughly that evidence of Paleo-Indians in Alberta has largely eluded detection. Many sites from this time period may be deeply buried; that is why discoveries such as the Fletcher site are so significant. (Much to the envy of Alberta archaeologists, less glacially-disturbed landscapes in Wyoming and Nebraska have revealed numerous signs of these early hunters.)

No Ice, Smaller Buffalo

The early communal hunters who appeared at the Fletcher site were adapting to changes occurring all over North America. The great mammoths and other big game which early people once hunted had disappeared. The southwest portions of North America, now part of such states as New Mexico and Arizona, started to turn into desert. People in these areas began to depend more on small game, and on various plant foods.

In the Eastern Woodlands, an area stretching south and east of Manitoba and Wisconsin to the Atlantic, walnut trees began to grow in areas where mammoths once wandered. People turned for survival to deer, rabbits and other small game as well as gathering nuts and other vegetable foods.

On the Northern Plains, scientists know that a distinct warming trend had begun. They also know the change in seasons became more dramatic because Arctic air was pulled down into Alberta for the first time with the separation of the Laurentide and Cordilleran ice.

During the same time period, starting about 11,000 years ago and ending about 8,000 years ago, another monumental change occurred. For reasons which are little understood, bison became smaller, and this likely resulted in a change in their social system. The enormous 600-kilogram bison of today are only about two-thirds the size of their hefty ancestors. The larger fossil specimens probably represent extremes within the population of a single species, and "cannot, in my opinion, be viewed as separate species," according to Michael Wilson of the University of Lethbridge's Department of Geology.

The bisons' once-flaring horns began to wane around the same time that mammoths died out. The reduction in their lethal headgear could help explain why buffalo had a stronger tendency to live in herds after the Ice Age. With smaller horns, they were simply less dangerous to each other and, as biologists say, became more "gregarious."

The ramifications for human hunters are clear. Once bison began to live in large herds, they became much more attractive targets for communal hunts.

The economy of Alberta's Plains likely revolved around bison for the last 10,000 years. Pinning down the beginnings of communal bison hunting — a strategy that profoundly affected social organization, settlement patterns and survival itself — is therefore a key challenge in Plains archaeology.

The attraction buffalo held for prehistoric people is easy to understand. Perhaps the modern-day equivalent to killing a bison would be winning a free hour's shopping in a supermarket, except that luck had less to do with the prehistoric hunt. Two bison, after all, provided as much meat as twenty antelope. Meat from one bison might supply a single hunter with food for at least two months. They provided prehistoric bands with almost everything they needed, from meat (dried for later use) to shelter, rough clothing and containers (from their hides) to cutlery and other tools (shaped

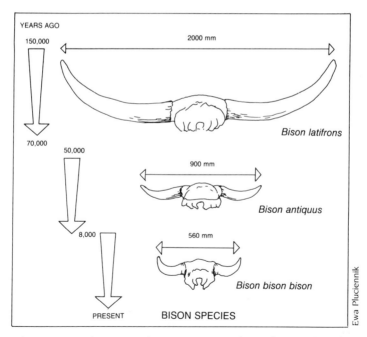

Evolutionary reduction in horn core size of North American bison (to scale).

from their bones). Although prehistoric people hunted elk, antelope, deer, muskrat, beaver, badger, fox and other game, nothing else could come close to providing the pay-off received from bison.

Dog Days on the Plains

What were the lives of these hunters like? Unfortunately, so few Early Prehistoric sites have been discovered in Alberta that we are forced to look to the American Plains, and to living groups of hunter-gatherers, to try to flesh out the picture. Even then, it is a highly speculative one.

Alberta archaeologists believe the plains people lived in small, mobile bands. They moved camp up to fifty times a year and traded with other bands over great distances, sometimes hundreds of kilometres. They met with these other bands occasionally to hunt communally, to exchange information and to arrange marriages.

These bands did not roam haphazardly across the landscape. To do so on the plains could have been suicide. The bands needed to be familiar enough with the habits of the buffalo so that they could intercept the herds by moving into the areas where they were likely to be at certain times. They needed water and shelter, and wood for fuel. They tailored their movements by the season, journeying to the woods in the winter and onto the plains in summer. Such a cycle is called a *seasonal round.*

Some early hunters may have moved off Alberta's Plains and into surrounding woods in winter even before the time of the Fletcher site. At Sibbald Creek, in the forested foothills west of Calgary, discoveries indicate that a group of four to six families hunted bison there more than 10,000 years ago. Early styles of spear points and poorly-preserved animal bones were found at the site.

Because prehistoric plains people did not stay in one place long, their campsites are rather difficult to detect. The places where they killed and butchered game or *kill sites*, are easier to discover, because many animal bones were left behind.

Dogs, the first animals to be domesticated, served as their beasts of burden. These dogs likely evolved from the wolf and may have accompanied the first hunters across Beringia. Each plains family may have had at least ten. Belongings were transported from camp to camp by dog-pulled travois, a method continued for perhaps thousands of years in this wheel-less society. The dogs were attached to poles joined by a frame. Goods were stashed onto the frame and one end of the poles dragged along the ground. A most useful technique when there were no roads!

Speaking of a later Plains period, John Ewers, in *The Blackfeet: Raiders of the Northwestern Plains*, writes: "When elderly Blackfoot Indians refer to this pre-horse period, they commonly identify it by the expression 'when we had only dogs for moving camp.'"

Prehistoric people made warm clothing out of fur and hide. Leather moccasins protected their feet from deadly frostbite. Only with such adaptations could early hunters have hoped to withstand the cold Alberta winter.

They likely used awls and needles made from bone to sew leggings, leather dresses and breech-cloths. Both sexes probably wore buffalo robes.

What did Paleo-Indians use for shelter? Evidence from Vermilion Lakes suggests they may have fashioned dome shelters out of hide and wood. Tipis, a more sophisticated form of shelter, probably were not developed until later.

Plains people had fire but were not always able to find wood. Dried buffalo chips (dung) had to do — and there was no shortage of that. Chips do not burn as well as wood, however, and smoke terribly in windless areas. Plains people likely sought sheltered areas in winter for their ready supply of wood.

Archaeologists have found evidence that humans in the Early Prehistoric, preserved meat by freezing. Piles of mammoth bones found at sites in Wyoming suggest that slabs of meat were once stacked and frozen. By 7,500 years ago, vast quantities of fire-broken rock, smashed-up bone and boiling pits appear in the archaeological record. They indicate that grease was extracted from the bones, probably to pound up with dry meat into pemmican.

Early people may also have dried meat in strips. Flesh from two bison could yield about forty-five kilograms of dried meat. The weight of meat can be reduced up to ten times by drying and it will keep for many months.

Prehistoric people butchered carcasses with stone tools. A sharpened stone was used for cutting and a *chopper*, made from bison tibia, was wielded to break muscle attachments.

Archaeologists, who are among the few modern-day people to continue the art of stone and bone tool-making, attest that such tools can be as effective as sharp steel knives if they are in the hands of a skilled practitioner.

These early Albertans were probably voracious meat-eaters. Evidence from fur-trading times suggests that men may have consumed up to three kilograms of meat per day, depending on availability, while women and children ingested up to two kilograms.

Depiction of Plains camp.

Few vegetables were available on the plains, although wild varieties of prairie turnips, onions, carrots, celery and berries may have been dug up or picked to supplement their diet in summer. We know from historic accounts that plants were later used for medicinal purposes. There is no indication that prehistoric Albertans practiced agriculture, except for possible tobacco plots (see the Cluny Site, Chapter 4).

Based on historic records at the time of contact, it is believed that prehistoric Natives probably decorated their bodies with ochre-based paints for ceremonial purposes and sewed beads of bone or seeds and used quills to decorate their clothing. Few remnants of such perishables survive.

Nor have we any definite knowledge of early religious practices. Belief in the powers of the supernatural, however, go back at least 30,000 years in human development. The later appearance on the plains of vision quest sites, rock art, stone cairns and circles called *medicine wheels*, suggest a deep dimension in prehistoric spirituality which so far eludes interpretation by the archaeological record alone.

Puzzle of the Altithermal

Argument swirls in archaeological circles about the effect of the early *Altithermal* on the Alberta Plains. The word refers to a climatic period between 8,000 and 4,500 years ago which was warmer and drier than today's conditions.

Originally it was thought that the Altithermal rendered the plains uninhabitable and that the Cody people packed their travois and moved out completely.

Today, that is no longer believed to be true. Records of human occupation during this time have been unearthed at Boss Hill in central Alberta, the Stampede site in the Cypress Hills, the Hawkwood site within the city of Calgary, and at a few other places.

Scientists have also revised their view of climatic conditions during this time. They now think the greatest period of warming occurred about 11,000 years ago, not 8,000 years ago as previously thought. The northern hemisphere summer occurred while the earth was closer to the sun than it has been ever since. It is now recognized that although the warming occurred 11,000 years ago, it took another several thousand years for its full impact to be felt on the plains. During that time, the lakes in the southern part of the province dried up. By 4,000 years ago, the climate became similar to today's.

What happened 11,000 years ago is explained by the *Milankovitch theory* of orbital tilt. Summer occurs when one hemisphere is tilted towards the sun and thus receives more daylight heating. Independent of this tilt is the location of the planet in its orbit. Thus the earth is close to the sun at one point (*perihelion*) and far away from the sun at the opposite point in its orbit (*aphelion*). Since there is a wobble in the tilt of the earth, there is a cycle when the northern summer occurs while the earth is in close approach to the sun, followed by northern summers when the earth is further from the sun.

About 11,000 years ago, the northern summer occurred (*axis tilt*) when the planet was at perihelion, and thus received the maximum amount of northern summer heating possible. Climate change induced by this relationship between orbit and tilt is the Milankovitch theory.

Two major schools of thought exist on what happened on the plains in the Altithermal. According to the first theory, the drought had such a disastrous effect on the bison range that plains people retreated to sources of water, such as the foothills and mountains, the Cypress Hills area or valleys of permanent rivers such as the South Saskatchewan, Bow and Red Deer.

The alternative theory is that although the plains did dry out, the results were far from catastrophic since the grasslands expanded northwards. Undoubtedly great fluctuations occurred from area to area and from year to year. The net effect may have been no loss of significant bison range in Alberta, although people would have congregated near water sources.

Many archaeologists are optimistic that the mystery of plains occupation during the Altithermal can be solved. Artifacts from this sketchy time period may be buried beneath one, two or twenty metres of earth.

Welcome!

Username: LACLIB999
Password: K337942M
    Price: 0
    Usage: 60 minute(s)

ESSID:
 Lacombe Library
Shared WEP Keys
(HEX 40 bit):
  1:
  2:
  3:
  4:

Valid to use until:
  2009/01/01 15:35:02

      Thank You!

917

New Points, New People?

Towards the end of the Early Prehistoric Period, more clues appear about Alberta's early occupants. Traces of hunters who used smaller, notched dart points show up for the first time in the archaeological record.

These reduced dart points may indicate the first appearance of the spear-thrower or *atlatl*, on the plains. These devices acted as extensions of the human arm and gave spears more range and force. The spears likely became smaller, and were feathered like arrows are today, hence their name, *darts*. Since the dart was smaller than the earlier spear, smaller points were necessary. (Once plains people had the atlatl, they could carry more weapon tips with them simply because they were smaller.)

The Boss Hill site, near Stettler in central Alberta, and the Hawkwood site, on Nose Hill in Calgary, represent the earliest occurrences of these smaller side-notched points on the Alberta Plains. Both are dated at between 8,000 and 7,500 years of age.

Boss Hill is significant because both the large, Early Prehistoric Period style of spear points and the smaller atlatl points have been found in the same deposits. This leads archaeologists to believe that the people who occupied Boss Hill were making the transition to this new technology. It also suggests the new weapon styles resulted from the arrival of new ideas, not a displacement of people.

Danek Mozdzenski

Manner of using atlatl.

"The Boss Hill site provides evidence of a Pre-Archaic culture phase in the central Alberta parklands," says Maurice Doll, of the Provincial Museum of Alberta. "The Pre-Archaic is described as a transitional phase between the late Paleo-Indian and Early Plains Archaic traditions. It is characterized by the coincidence of lanceolate and notched projectile points."

Two hearths have been unearthed at the site, along with the remains of four bison, one badger, one muskrat, two geese, two ducks and various other game. Prehistoric hunters appear to have camped there in late summer or fall.

The Hawkwood site, found in the midst of what is now a housing subdivision on Nose Hill, provides a glimpse at some of the first known Calgarians. The camp appears to have been occupied by one or two families who left behind two small hearths, bison bones and some stone tool debris. The camp is situated in an exposed spot, indicating that the families probably used it only in milder weather.

What is the significance of Hawkwood? The predominance of buffalo bones at both sites strongly suggests that the Altithermal did not change the bison-based economy of the plains. It seems other game still played a minor role next to buffalo.

The Enigma of the Notched Dart Points

Archaeologists have no concrete explanation for the variety of notched lance tips which show up in the transition period between the Early and Middle Prehistoric Period, around 7,500 years ago.

It might indicate the spread of a new weapon style into the last Paleo-Indian population, probably from the Eastern Woodlands. Or, entirely new populations may have moved onto the plains. Since late styles of Early Prehistoric points are associated with Early Middle Prehistoric notched points at Boss Hill and Hawkwood, some archaeologists suspect this to be a case of diffusion.

There are other questions. Did the Paleo-Indians, with their bigger lance tips, simply vanish? Or did they retreat northward, until they found more hospitable conditions such as the presence of caribou herds? The puzzle is tangled and fascinating.

The Mummy Cave Complex

The next players on the plains created Mummy Cave assemblages, named after a cave east of Yellowstone National Park where they left artifacts. These were new varieties of side-notched weapon points including Bitterroot and Salmon River.

Archaeologists disagree on whether the different styles of weapon points used by Mummy Cave point-makers indicate a number of different cultural groups or not. As Anthony Buchner of the Historic Resources Branch of Manitoba has noted, Mummy Cave represents a continuation of the basic technology and way of life already practiced on the plains for thousands of years.

The Stampede site at the base of the Cypress Hills is one of the most promising Mummy Cave sites in Alberta. Amazingly, excavations of an area only seven metres square turned up almost 5,000 samples of debris from prehistoric tool manufacture. Bitterroot or Blackwater side-notched points dating back more than 7,000 years were also found. Unfortunately, wet conditions prevented archaeologists from excavating further.

Stampede is believed to have been a semi-permanent camp, used repeatedly. From an archaeological point of view, both Stampede and Hawkwood are significant because of the large

(Right) Boss Hill
Approximately
7,900 years ago
(Far right) Bitterroot
Approximately
7,500 -4,000 years ago

Danek Mozdzenski

Two examples of projectile points (shown actual size) of the Middle Prehistoric Period.

number of buffalo bones found there. The sites were occupied at a time when archaeologists once thought the plains were deserted, or that people had to shift their subsistence from buffalo to smaller game because of the effect of the drier climate on grazing patterns.

Yet in terms of meat weight, buffalo probably accounted for ninety per cent of the meat consumed even at Boss Hill, where a greater variety of animal bones were found than at either Stampede or Hawkwood. This suggests that in this period of increased aridity, sufficient buffalo continued grazing on the plains, therefore, the people did not have to alter their dependence on buffalo-hunting.

McKean and Oxbow

Other clues about Middle Prehistoric life are found in two new styles of weapons which emerged on the Alberta Plains between 5,000 and 3,500 years ago. These are called the *Oxbow* and *McKean Complexes.*

(Right) Oxbow
Approximately
4,600 -3,000 years ago
(Far right) McKean Phase
Approximately
4,200 -3,000 years ago

Danek Mozdzenski

Two examples of projectile points (shown actual size) of the Middle Prehistoric Period.

Oxbow points, used between about 5,000 and 3,000 years ago, featured dart tips with large corner-notches and indented bases.

Some archaeologists, such as Brian Reeves of the University of Calgary, speculate from the style of the Oxbow point that it represents a development from the earlier Mummy Cave material. Perhaps a group of people who used the earlier Mummy Cave points gradually changed the style until they became Oxbow points. Rod Vickers confirms this speculation.

"It suggests an 'in situ' development of the culture, and also it seems to be one of the first cultures that is more common in the Northern Plains than elsewhere.

"In a way, it shows that the Saskatchewan basin area, at least on a gross scale, was different than what was going on elsewhere."

Oxbow sites are more common than any of the earlier sites — approximately ninety are known. They occur on the plains and later in the forests.

Finds in Saskatchewan indicate that Oxbow people were communal bison-hunters. Perhaps most important, the Oxbow people left the first tantalizing evidence of distinct ethnic groupings among prehistoric cultures on the plains. That evidence is found at the Gray site, a mass Oxbow graveyard near Swift Current in southwestern Saskatchewan. Prehistoric people transported and buried their dead at the site over an astounding time span of 2,000 years. Imagine a contemporary graveyard that has been used for 2,000 years.

The McKean Complex, composed of three different styles of projectile points (McKean, Duncan and Hanna) shows a different style of weaponry appearing on the Alberta Plains by 4,200 years ago. The McKean and Duncan styles are unnotched at the sides, but deeply notched at the bottom. This suggests that points were hafted in a different manner. Perhaps this approach had advantages, or perhaps it was just a different custom, rather like the style changes in beer bottles.

The Hanna point, which becomes more common in the later McKean sites, has corner-notches which probably indicate a change in how the tip was attached to the dart shaft. This is similar to styles dating back to about 1,000 years earlier in Wyoming.

These styles are very similar to those found on the other side of the Rockies, in the Great Basin area of the United States. Such a distribution pattern suggests an expansion of a group of people from the Wyoming-Rocky Mountain area up into Alberta.

Both Oxbow and McKean points are found in Alberta, however, in a subsequent period. This may suggest that two different cultures managed to exist side by side. There are simply not enough data to tell.

We know little about either the Oxbow or McKean users.

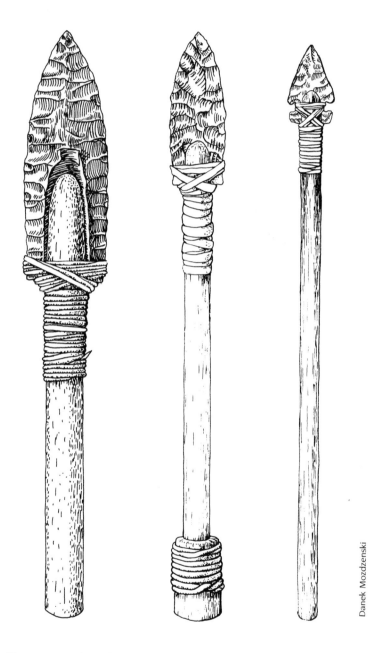

Three examples of hafted points. Clovis (left), McKean (middle) and Plains Side-Notched (right).

Brian Reeves argues that McKean hunters drove the Oxbow people off the plains, although many others believe the two co-existed on the Northern Plains for several hundreds of years.

Did the people who used McKean points hunt buffalo communally? The most extensive McKean campsite yet excavated on the Alberta Plains suggests they did. Cactus Flower, a camp dating back to 4,000 or 3,500 years ago, is situated north of Medicine Hat where the South Saskatchewan River has cut deep, sheer cliffs. Near the camp, more gentle slopes provide game with access to the river, the only nearby source of water.

It has been suggested that at Cactus Flower, the people who used McKean points may have employed a different hunting technique than the bison jumps seen in Mummy Cave sites.

The reasoning goes this way: the Cactus Flower site is situated by one of the few spots along that stretch of the river which can be forded. Archaeologists therefore surmise that McKean hunters may simply have ambushed buffalo as they went down to drink at the river. This represents a markedly different subsistence technique than that associated with buffalo jumps.

John Brumley, a Medicine Hat-based archaeological consultant, identified ten occupations at Cactus Flower, including two fairly sparse occupations by people who later used Pelican Lake points. The numerous levels at the site allow archaeologists to look at very small changes in styles of projectile points, although interpreting style preference is difficult.

Eventually, use of the Cactus Flower campsite began to decline. Later, people may have become so proficient at using pounds and bison jumps — witness Head-Smashed-In — that they no longer employed the ambushing technique.

No Easy Tricks to Communal Bison Hunting

Buffalo only look like lumbering dolts. Actually, they are skittish, speedy and relatively agile. They can detect humans up to six kilometres away. They have been clocked at speeds approaching sixty kilometres an hour. Not exactly lumbering.

Although people have stalked and chased buffalo on Alberta's Plains for about 10,000 years, the technique of rounding them up still isn't easy. Today, breeders of commercial stock use motorized vehicles with metal wings to herd them. Unlike cattle, bison strenuously resist entering gates.

How did prehistoric people manage without electric cattle prods, two-way radios, and most especially, without horses? They were, after all, on foot.

Instead of relying on the speed of horses or on deadly technology, the first Albertans had to use their powers of keen observation and thorough knowledge of bison behaviour. If you want to catch a bison, you have to think like a bison. They knew too, that once the hunter got in close, both beast (and hunter) were vulnerable. They had to act fast.

But first they had to get close. The slightest provocation can drive a seemingly calm herd wild, a threat prehistoric people took elaborate precautions against. From historic accounts, we know they levied harsh punishments against persons who disrupted herds before communal hunts. Such "criminals," in Native justice systems, were often whipped or had their tipis and possessions destroyed. The point was to publicly humiliate the wrongdoer, though the tribe might replace destroyed possessions within a few days.

Most important, prehistoric hunters made ingenious use of the landscape. At first, they used simple surrounds, or trapped bison in gullies. Later they devised two other methods: running them over cliffs (*buffalo jumps*) and tricking them into corrals (*buffalo pounds*).

Each method required careful preparation. Bison will not willingly crowd into a corral. An elaborate

series of stone cairns and ramps had to be devised
to trick the buffalo. Ramps sloping down to hidden
pounds, for example, might be packed with snow
and covered with water to make them slippery, so
that trapped bison could not escape.

Once trapped in a gully or pound, bison could still
put up a fight. Because of their pear shape — bigger
at the head than the tail — they are able to squeeze
through fairly small openings. Once they got their
shoulders partly through a hole in an improvised log
"fence," for example, they could easily extricate
themselves and were almost impossible to stop on
foot.

"The buffalo will never give up but will continue
to struggle until completely exhausted," notes
George Frison in *Prehistoric Hunters of the High Plains.*

Hunting bison could not be undertaken without
considerable strategy — until the arrival of the
horse and gun. The prehistoric hunter showed a lot
more savvy than the gun-toting cowboy.

Alberta's Mysterious Medicine Wheels

Stone by stone, for perhaps 5,000 years, prehistoric people added to a dome of rocks on a high
hill near Bassano in southern Alberta. They
fashioned twenty-six to twenty-eight spokes radiating
from the central cairn, then enclosed the spokes
within a circle.

Was the medicine wheel used for religious
ceremonies? Or for commemorating events or persons? Could it even have been part of prehistoric
astronomy?

Archaeologists are not really sure. What they do
know is that Alberta contains two-thirds of the
world's known medicine wheels. About forty-five
medicine wheels have been discovered in the
province, usually situated on top of high hills. Sometimes central cairns consist only of a few rocks;
sometimes they are hefty piles of stones. Sometimes
they feature only four spokes, sometimes only concentric circles with no spokes at all.

The first published account of medicine wheels was by George Dawson who, in 1885, described Sundial Hill, about forty-five kilometres north of Lethbridge:

"A point of note to the Indians in this region is that called Sun-dial Hill by Mr. Nelson. There is here a cairn with concentric circles of stones and radiating lines. I have not seen it, and therefore cannot describe it in detail. It is named Onoka-katzi and regarded with much reverence."

The medicine wheels at Sundial Hill and at Majorville are among the most elaborate. At Majorville, the boulder pile in the middle is nine metres wide and contained ceremonial stones. The cairn was initially used in Oxbow times about 5,000 years ago and it appears to have been employed almost continuously until historic times. Does such prolonged use indicate the existence of an ancient and stable ceremonial tradition on the Alberta Plains?

What is clear is that medicine wheels come in a

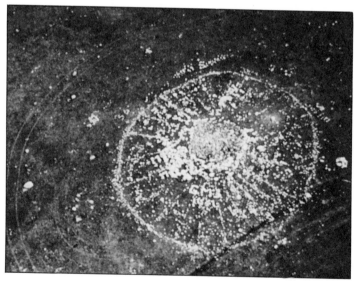

Air photo of the Majorville cairn.

bewildering variety of shapes. But one archaeologist who has studied medicine wheels in detail, archaeological consultant John Brumley, says attempting to compare and relate these diverse structures simply because they fall into the general class of medicine wheels is "like discussing aspirin and penicillin together simply because they are both drugs.

"The result has been an extremely muddled picture of just what medicine wheels are and what we do and do not know about them."

Like many archaeologists, Michael Wilson of the University of Lethbridge's Department of Geology believes these mysterious stone arrangements had multiple uses, "and we can be certain that specific uses were but surface expressions of deep, underlying cultural structures beyond the research of the archaeologist."

According to some Native sources, medicine wheels are commemorative monuments to individuals. The lines illustrate the war deeds of a dead chief, and rocks piled at the end of a line represent warriors he has killed. For example, Many Spotted Horses Medicine Wheel, on the Blood Indian Reserve near Lethbridge, is said to be a commemorative wheel to a Blood war chief.

Medicine wheels may also have been used in vision-questing. One Crow legend from the time of Lewis and Clark tells of Chief Red Plume visiting a medicine wheel in hopes of receiving a vision which would strengthen his prowess as a warrior. On his fourth night of fasting at the site, he was visited by three small men and one small woman who lived in the underground passage to the wheel. He stayed with them for three days and learned the arts of warfare and leadership. Red Plume eventually became a powerful leader who upon his death, specified that his spirit would occupy a shrine at the medicine wheel.

Another theory holds that medicine wheels, like Stonehenge, are part of a prehistoric "calendar" and the stones are designed to align celestial bodies at summer solstice. Some see a link between summer solstice, medicine wheels and the so-called "sun dances" or "thirst dances" of plains bands. Unfortunately, many alignments do not work.

One of the great mysteries of Alberta archaeology, in other words, is still unsolved.

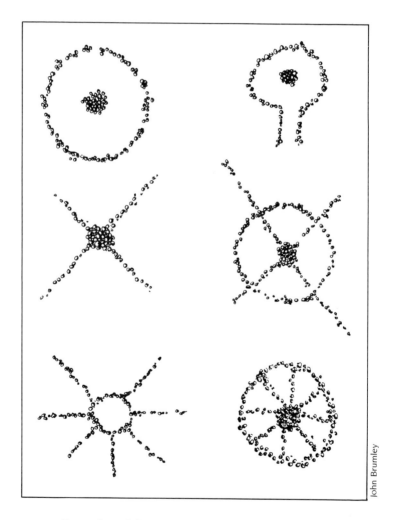

Examples of the major types of medicine wheels.

A Prehistoric Graveyard Tells a Tale

At the same time that ancient Egyptians were embalming their dead to prepare them for afterlife, hunters on the Western Canadian Plains were carrying the bones of their dead from camp to camp in *bundle bags*.

The hunters were gradually making their way to the band's traditional burial grounds in southwestern Saskatchewan. The problem was dead bodies were too heavy and awkward to transport as they were, and death often occurred far away from the cemetery. (Archaeologists estimate one person died every nine months in a fifty-person band.)

The answer was to lighten the load. Corpses were placed on high scaffolds in trees. There the flesh withered with exposure or was picked away by insects, small animals and birds. Feasting and fasting by close relatives may have accompanied the placement of the dead on the scaffold.

Bones were then packaged into bundle bags — sometimes bones of different individuals were mistakenly placed in the same bag. These bags were taken by dog travois to a mass cemetery, a journey that might cover hundreds of kilometres.

These glimpses at prehistoric burial habits on the plains stem from archaeological work at the Gray site, a mass cemetery near Swift Current, Saskatchewan. In the 1970s, archaeologists found ninety-nine graves, containing the remains of 304 individuals.

The tools uncovered clearly identify the burial ground as belonging to Oxbow people, who also occupied Alberta at the same time. They were active traders. Shells from the Pacific and copper from the Great Lakes region have been unearthed at the Gray site.

Most remarkable, radiocarbon dating techniques show the cemetery was used continuously for at least 2,200 years, until about 3,000 years ago. This hints of continuous ethnic traditions (or similarities in beliefs and values) among scattered groups of nomadic hunters on the plains.

Archaeologists found puzzling differences in the wear and decomposition of bones at the Gray site which could not be explained by age. Cut-marks were discovered on heavily-weathered bones which suggested artificial dismemberment. Explanation? Some individuals died months before burial and had their bones carried to the site.

Before burying their dead, the Oxbow people often performed other procedures. They broke bones (other than the skull) into smaller pieces. Sometimes they removed the articular ends of long bones from the fleshless corpses and rubbed them with ground ochre. Archaeologists believe they may have been afraid of evil spirits returning from the dead. Breaking the bones and treating them with potions may have been seen as a way of reducing the "mobility" of the soul.

Rodent teeth, eagle talons and dog bones were also found at the cemetery. Were they offerings to the gods?

"According to some ethnographic accounts, the dog limb bones may represent assistance in the transport of the soul in its journey," writes Jim Millar in the *Canadian Journal of Archaeology*.

Relatively few prehistoric burial sites have been discovered in Alberta. Today, because of the growing (and understandable) sensitivity of Native groups, graves are rarely dug up, although they have sometimes been revealed accidentally.

It seems clear, however, that prehistoric people did not always bury their dead. They sometimes left them in scaffolds on trees or in rocks or caves. With few exceptions, their graves betray no traces of a society where one individual enjoyed considerably more status than another.

The Weapons of the Plains

The life of the prehistoric plains hunter depended to a large extent on the efficiency and reliability of his weapons. Techniques of honing and refining tools to his advantage were developed over thousands of years.

It was not enough for prehistoric hunters to lure bison into a trap if, at the critical moment, their spear tips failed to penetrate the animal's hide. Their immediate physical safety, and ultimately, a band's survival, demanded fine craftsmanship in the art of weapon-making.

Early Prehistoric Period — 11,500 to 7,500 years ago. The first-known people to occupy the plains carried heavy spears tipped with long stone points. These points were *hafted* or attached in a socket or notch at the end of a wooden shaft. Sinew or a sticky material, such as pitch, was used to bind the tip in place.

This was not as simple a matter as it might sound. First, the point had to be sharp enough to penetrate the animal's hide. The blade edges then had to gouge a hole large enough to allow the point to reach the vital organs. If the blade edges were not wide enough, or the shaft and binding too large, the rest of the weapon could not be driven through the hole made by the projectile point. The binding, moreover, had to be securely fastened — but not so cumbersome that it could not penetrate the hide.

It is believed Paleo-Indians refined their spears by the use of a foreshaft, rather than simply mounting points at the end of their main spears. In this way, hunters could carry several foreshafts as well as a single mainshaft. This allowed them to easily pull the main spear out of a dead animal — a useful feature if they wanted to kill another animal right away, or had to protect themselves.

Middle Prehistoric Period — 7,500 to 1,750 years ago. The people who lived in Alberta during this time

Danek Mozdzenski

The spear-thrower or atlatl acted as an extension of the arm and propelled spears (darts) significantly further and with more force.

likely *threw* spears or darts rather than carry and thrust them. They used the *atlatl* — a spear-throwing device which is basically an extension of the arm.

The atlatl consists of a stick with a handle on one end and a hook at the other. The hunter holds the handle and attaches a socket in a small spear called a dart. He then thrusts the atlatl forward; the dart detaches and hurls ahead, gaining extra propulsion because the atlatl increased the length and power of the hunter's throw. Hunters could bring down large animals with atlatls from a distance of as much as seventy metres.

A further refinement consisted of weighting the atlatl to add velocity or accuracy. The method of weighting was also practiced by Aztecs and Australian aborigines.

Late Prehistoric Period — 1,750 years ago to A.D. 1750. This period is characterized by small, notched or triangular points thought to have been hafted to arrows propelled by bows. The bow and arrow provided a more portable and flexible weaponry to plains hunters; bundles of light arrows could easily be carried on a hunt, and hunters could take aim either standing or kneeling. Later, after the introduction of the horse, Plains Indians continued to use the bow and arrow to hunt bison, often in preference to early, unreliable rifles, which were cumbersome to reload.

Mark Chez

The bow and arrow proved a valuable tool for the Plains Indians.

Why Buffalo Chips Are Badly Underrated

Intrepid Alberta archaeologists have actually supervised "buffalo chip" experiments to gain insight into their burning properties. At Head-Smashed-In Buffalo Jump, for example, no wood fuel was available in the immediate area for prehistoric hunters, although there is ample evidence of fire from the thousands of fire-broken rock fragments archaeologists have found there.

"The common presumption in such a circumstance is that an alternate fuel, such as bison chips, was used, and this can be verified by experimental archaeology," says Milt Wright, an archaeologist with the ASA.

He conducted several field experiments using bison chip fuel and boiling stone technology. He concluded: "Although roundly criticized for their poor heat yield and smoky nature, chips do in fact produce abundant heat, albeit of a non-radiant variety, and are particularly well-suited for heating rock for stone-boiling."

Hot Rocks

Question: How do you boil water for grease extraction when you don't have a pot?

Answer: Dig a hole, line it with a waterproof hide, then fill it with water and smashed-up bone. Build a fire beside the boiling pit and heat rocks in the fire. Dip the hot rocks in the water and presto — boiling water.

Head-Smashed-In Buffalo Jump. Terrified and unable to stop in time, the buffalo hurtle over the cliff to meet certain death.

4

Archaeology of the Plains Indians: Head-Smashed-In

The pounding of hooves mixes with wild shrieks on the wind-scoured Porcupine Hills of southern Alberta. Through the dust, an observer can make out hundreds of buffalo, eyes wide with panic, thundering across the short-grass prairie. On either side of them, a human wall of more than a hundred hunters waves and shouts and screams, trying to keep the frenzied half-ton animals heading in the same direction. The herd could easily swing off course into the thin human line, goring or trampling a few puny hunters in their path. In the next few seconds, the fate of perhaps 300 buffalo and the immediate future of more than 200 hunters, wives, children and medicine men will be conclusively decided. For the hunters, it is both knowledge and magic — that may or may not work. This is the place called Head-Smashed-In.

To the east, the grasslands seem to extend forever. To the west crests the spine of the rolling, treeless Porcupine Hills. Members of five nomadic bands have been here for days mustering every supernatural and human power they know to make the hunt a success.

Medicine men and medicine women, dressed in buffalo skins and feather headdresses, have chanted and invoked their gods. They have mimicked the hunt by tossing a small stone shaped like a buffalo (called "iniskim") into the air and catching it in a hide blanket. If the magic works, the real buffalo will similarly fall to their deaths. For at Head-Smashed-In, the rolling prairie suddenly falls away, although you can't see the change until you get close. That is what the hunters are counting on, although the issue is by no means clear. Will the bison jump or will they turn? The rituals may give the hunters an edge, so they continue unceasingly all through the hunt.

Three trained "buffalo runners" left the camp days ago. They know the huge beasts often graze by the thousands in the lush valleys of the Porcupine Hills. Their job is to move the buffalo from the huge natural gathering basin above the cliffs for the final stampede.

They stay downwind and disguise themselves with the skins of antelopes and wolves, animals which bison usually tolerate at close range. One ploy is for "wolves" to harass calves that have strayed in the direction of the jump. The natural tendency of adult buffalo is to come to the calves' protection, thereby gradually edging the rest of the herd toward the cliffs. The runners must be careful not to startle the beasts; one whiff of human scent and the buffalo could disappear in the wrong direction.

One buffalo runner tries an even more remarkable tactic. He disguises himself as a buffalo calf and mimics the plaintive bleats of a calf separated from its mother. The entire herd, composed mostly of cows and calves, turns to follow him in the direction of the distant cliffs.

Runners need other knowledge, however, to manipulate the herds over more than ten kilometres. An elaborate system of prehistoric stone markers, called "drive lanes," has been piled up as a guide to keep the herds headed towards the cliffs.

The roundup takes three days. At last the weary buffalo hunters succeed in luring the animals into the area above the cliff. Now they have to do more than simply drive the unpredictable beasts in a certain direction. They must manoeuvre the animals precisely to a particular spot near the cliff top only 100 metres wide. The pace increases. Fresh hunters join the runners. They shout and scream to the swelling thunder of hooves. A medicine man chants.

As they near the edge, only about a dozen of the tightly-packed buffalo can actually see where they are headed. The others pound blindly behind them. Group fear and momentum seems greater than the sum of its parts. Yet the bison could still veer off course; the hunt could still fail.

This time, the magic proves potent. The herd speeds up a small slope, less than a kilometre above the cliffs. At the top, as planned, the lead animals can only see prairie stretching endlessly below. They are the victims of an optical illusion — particular to this spot on the slope — which prevents them from perceiving the drop ahead.

The buffalo keep running. Now their physical shape is against them. On downhill runs, their small back legs can't cope well with their massive front weight. Unable to stop in time, they hurtle helplessly over the cliff and crash fifteen metres below.

Judith Nickol

One ploy of the buffalo runners was to disguise themselves as wolves.

Many of the beasts are killed; others are wounded or stunned. Hunters stationed below waste no time, for they believe survivors will go back to the herds and warn them of the trap, one of the reasons hunts fail, they believe. They kill the wounded animals with sharp stone-tipped spears, arrows delivered from bows, and large stone hammers.

When all is still, the long, satisfying process of butchering and processing begins. Now, almost all band members, including women and children who probably helped line the drive lanes in the final stages of the hunt, join in. Stomachs are sliced open. The heavy hide is cut back from the meat and fat to promote cooling and prevent spoilage.

Hungry butchers slice off snacks. Tongues, eyeballs, livers, kidneys and brains are favoured treats often consumed while butchering. Most of the meat, however, will be dried and made into pemmican — a mixture of animal fat, meat and sometimes berries — then stored in hide containers for the winter months ahead. Chill winds are beginning to rage down from the mountains.

No one knows how many times prehistoric hunters enacted a similar scenario at Head-Smashed-In, the first buffalo jump used in what is now Alberta.

Following the hunt, the buffalo is butchered and processed. Most of the meat is dried and made into pemmican.

At least 5,500 years ago, prehistoric people began using the jump, west of the junction of the Oldman River and Willow Creek, near the present site of Fort Macleod. They continued until European culture, or more precisely, the horse, reached the plains around A.D. 1730 and changed the nature of the hunt forever. Tens of thousands of bison likely perished beneath those cliffs.

Dozens of other bison jumps are scattered throughout southern Alberta, and many more remain to be discovered. Finding the right cliff in buffalo country was not easy; each jump is a testimony to the prehistoric hunters' increasingly clever use of the landscape to hunt the animal on which his life most depended.

Head-Smashed-In is one of the oldest, largest, best-preserved and most extensively-used of all jumps in North America. Around 4,000 years ago, the site was mysteriously abandoned for about 1,000 years. Did new people, who for some reason did not use jumps, move into the area? Did the climate and vegetation change thereby driving buffalo away? Obviously, more research is required.

Newcomers on the Plains

By 3,000 years ago, the Alberta Plains probably looked much the way they did when Europeans arrived. The northern forests had pushed as far south; the grasslands which once extended as far north as the North Saskatchewan River had developed into mixed parkland forest.

New people may have infiltrated the plains, as Head-Smashed-In came into use again. These people possessed small, notched dart tips with barbs, a style archaeologists identify as characteristic of *Pelican Lake* (a site in south-central Saskatchewan). Such lance tips are a fairly common find in Alberta, suggesting the population density on the plains began to increase around 3,000 years ago.

Whoever they were, the makers of Pelican Lake points appear to have been the renaissance people of the plains. They carried tools made of exotic rocks, such as obsidian from Wyoming and chert (a form of flint) from Montana. Their horizons were perhaps broader; they enjoyed increased contact and trade with hunters in other areas. They focussed their hunting strategies on buffalo jumps.

Unlike their predecessors, the Pelican Lake users consistently left more definite signs of their temporary camps on the landscape, in the form of tipi rings. These circles of stones were probably laid around the outside of cone-shaped skin tents to hold the bottom flap on the ground, just as modern campers sometimes use stones when they run out of tent pegs. Hundreds of thousands of tipi rings, which archaeologists have mostly been unable to date, can still be discovered on the southern Alberta Plains.

Although they have been called the renaissance people of the plains, the Pelican Lake inhabitants likely possessed neither pottery nor the bow and arrow. Instead, they made do with the dart and spear-thrower. Some archaeologists believe smaller Pelican Lake points may indeed have been used for the bow and arrow.

Two New Groups on the Plains

Towards the end of the Middle Prehistoric Period, the people who used the Pelican Lake style of point seem to have vanished from the plains. Did they move to other areas, or simply change their weapon style?

No one knows for certain. However, archaeologists have determined that the plains were inhabited by people using two new styles of technology: *Besant* and *Avonlea*.

The Besant people are known as superb bison-hunters. They appear to have occupied a widespread area from the edge of the Eastern Woodlands of North America to the Rockies. They are identifiable by the heavy, somewhat crude corner-notched dart tips they employed and their frequent use of Knife River flint, a beautiful honey-coloured stone from a river by the same name in North Dakota.

The Besant people are credited with adding a new and important strategy to bison hunting: the pound. Buffalo were gathered into pounds in much the same way as they were lured over cliffs, using a system of runners and drive lanes. A major difference, however, was that successful jumps immediately killed or injured many animals, whereas pounds only contained them. Animals rounded up in pounds may have been kept alive for one or two days while Natives held religious celebrations giving thanks for their good fortune.

Pounds almost always made use of a slope of some kind to hide a makeshift "corral." A small step at the entrance to the corral, of less than a metre, helped contain the trapped animals. The corral walls were usually built of bits of wood and brush, and stood about the same height as the bison. For the pound to succeed, the flimsy walls had to appear solid, an illusion the Natives created by draping them with buffalo hides. As long as the hides represented a solid wall, the bison could be fooled. However, if any light were to shine through a hole in the hide, the buffalo could sense the ruse and easily break out.

Historic accounts tell of up to 1200 animals being kept in one pound at a time, and of two herds being brought in during one day. One witness to pounding techniques was Alex-

(Far left) Pelican Lake
Approximately
3,300-2,000 years ago
(Left) Besant
Approximately
2,100-1,200 years ago

Two examples of projectile points (shown actual size) from the Middle Prehistoric Period.

Danek Mozdzenski

ander Henry, the elder, who observed a buffalo runner disguised as a bison calf in 1776. He wrote: "Their gestures so closely resembled those of the animals themselves that had I not been in on the secret I should have been as much deceived as the buffalo."

Why use a pound instead of a jump? Terrain seems to have been the crucial factor. Pounds, which required a fair supply of wood, appear to have been used more in central Alberta, which receives more precipitation than the south and has more rolling terrain. Jumps, in contrast, tend to be found in dry, eroded areas, broken by river banks.

Who were the fine hunters who brought the pound into use on Alberta's plains? Were they simply the successors of the people who made Pelican Lake points?

The origins of Besant point-makers remain clouded, although a couple of hints surface in the puzzling archaeological record. Fragments of ceramics have been found at some Besant sites, such as the Ross Glen site southeast of Medicine Hat, excavated by Michael Quigg, then of the ASA. Finds from Ross Glen and the Wintering Hills south of Drumheller suggest ties with Manitoba and Saskatchewan people who were making the same kind of pottery around the same time. The extensive use of Knife River flint provides another clue and points to contacts with North and South Dakota, where people were employing similar tools.

The Dakota connection is intriguing for another reason. The use of burial mounds among the Dakota relatives of the Besant bison hunters is of interest to those Alberta archaeologists who want to learn more about the role of rank in early societies. Archaeologists find it significant that no grave goods have been unearthed from these burial mounds, since such

93

goods can sometimes be interpreted as a sign of an individual's rank or status in society.

Archaeology has determined that plains burials were extremely rare. For long periods in prehistory, plains people appear not to have buried their dead, but left them (as they did at the time of European contact) to the elements, perhaps on rocks or in trees. (See Chapter 3.)

Pelican Lake point-makers, however, appear to be an exception. About half a dozen burial sites have been found, including one of a young man near Okotoks and one near the southwest border. In all cases, grave goods accompanied the corpse. They included native copper, traded from the Great Lakes region more than 3,000 kilometres away, as well as drilled or perforated grizzly bear claws or incisors from elk or bison. Spiral shells from the Pacific Northwest, called dentalia, were also found at the Okotoks site.

These goods pose intriguing questions about status and rank in plains society. So far, they have yielded no answers. Alberta archaeologists lack the evidence to conclude from a few rare sites that certain individuals possessed greater status or rank. Who is to say that many individuals did not possess grizzly bear claws, they ask?

Alberta's archaeological record reveals only so much about social organization and religious beliefs, although rock art, medicine wheels and vision quest sites may someday reveal more. The early fur traders, however, found a high degree of egalitarianism among Native groups on the plains. Their accounts and those from contemporary studies of modern hunter-gatherers (in such remote areas as Africa's Kalihari Desert, the Australian outback and Canada's subarctic) provide the basis for our sketchy picture of prehistoric social organization on the plains.

Equality — The Byword on the Plains

Ethnographic studies of Plains Indians by scholars such as Hugh Dempsey, an assistant director with the Glenbow Museum, and research on hunter-gatherers around the world, give us a picture of what prehistoric plains society may have been like.

The small bands which roamed the plains likely consisted of between fifty to 100 people — perhaps three or four related couples, their parents, their children and some additional unrelated people. Bands probably met occasionally with other bands not only for communal hunts, but for large regional gatherings where they exchanged information and performed important religious ceremonies, perhaps similar to the mid-summer Sundance of historic times.

Band leaders were not really chosen; some individuals simply became leaders by virtue of long years of success in hunting or warfare, and by possessing the leadership qualities of wisdom, patience and generosity. Bands arrived at decisions through consensus among the older, more experienced, male members. The leader had no authoritarian control and members were free to leave one group to join another.

Status distinctions could, of course, be earned in prehistoric societies by serving the band well. Successful hunters would be recognized for their ability to provide for others; good shamen would gain favour by their ability to influence the spirit world.

Such status distinctions were relatively few, however, compared with European society, which seemed almost obsessed with rank. Skillful hunters, powerful medicine men and their relatives might enjoy the best cuts of meat in prehistoric plains society, but everyone would still receive their share. Personal property was kept to a minimum. People owned their own tipis, dogs, travois and bow and arrows, but not much more; the bounty of the hunt belonged to all.

E. Brown/Provincial Archives of Alberta

Sarsi woman with dog travois.

The equality of plains society almost certainly did not extend to women. The belief is that teenaged females entered into marriages arranged by their fathers. If a marriage did not work out, a woman could likely "divorce" her husband by returning to her family, who would accept her back again, depending on the circumstances.

Although women did not participate in band decision-making, they no doubt played many important roles in pre-historic life. They likely made and owned the tipis, sewed and decorated clothing, gathered wild plants, participated in the ceremonial/religious life of the group and possessed the most detailed knowledge of kin relationships.

No doubt their lives were full of drudgery, so much so that the impetus for polygamy may have originated with the wife who wanted another wife to help with the work.

The egalitarianism of the plains is in marked contrast to prehistoric life on the Northwest Coast. There, hereditary chiefs developed permanent villages with as many as 5,000 occupants and ruled over a class of slaves who catered to their whims.

Why the social contrast between the two regions? It can be argued that the nature of bison-hunting made status distinctions difficult on the plains. Survival depended on cooperating with other hunters to drive bison. In such a society, there was a lack of personal property because no one could really own more than any one else. After a communal hunt, for example, how could anyone tell which bison had been killed by which hunter?

Coastal societies, in contrast, often depended on access or rights of access to prime fishing areas, which could be inherited. Moreover, individuals who aspired to rank could simply move away from a camp and form their own semi-permanent village — an inconceivable option to the nomadic dwellers of the plains. Status on the plains appears to have become a force in Natives life only after individual bison-hunting became easier, in other words, after Europeans introduced the horse and gun.

An Arrow Strikes the Plains

The dart-throwing Besant users shared the plains with another group which made Avonlea points and used the bow and arrow.

Danek Mozdzenski

(Far left) Avonlea
Approximately
2,000 -800 years ago
(Centre) Plains Side-Notched
Approximately
1,200 -250 years ago
(Left) Prairie Side-Notched
Approximately
1,200 -250 years ago

Three examples of projectile points (shown actual size) from the Old Women's Phase of the Late Prehistoric Period.

Archaeologists can detect the arrival of the bow and arrow by the delicate, tiny points the Avonlea people made. Such fine points would clearly have been unsuitable for the heavier shafts of atlatl darts.

Where did Avonlea people come from? One theory, not widely accepted, holds that they were Athapaskan invaders who travelled south from the boreal forest to become the predecessors of the Navahos and Apaches of the American southwest. A more popular belief suggests they emerged from the same group which produced the people who made Pelican Lake points.

The bows and arrows they brought were lighter and more portable than spears. Bow hunters could take more shots than spear-throwers because they could carry a bundle of light arrows with them; they could also take aim from different positions, whether on foot or kneeling. Perhaps as a result of these advantages, the new weapon spread rapidly.

The remarkable Avonlea users also pioneered the first extensive use of pottery on the plains. This development made it possible for pots to be placed in a fire, not only making cooking easier, but greatly extending the range of culinary possibilities.

These long-ago craftsmen fashioned relatively simple, unpainted, coconut-shaped vessels. Little is known about the techniques these prehistoric potters used. We know, however, they did not employ potter's wheels.

Decoration was kept to a minimum, consisting mainly of circular depressions made by pushing a finger into the wet clay and a general texturing of the vessel surface by pressing knotted fabric against the clay.

For archaeologists, the vital aspect of ceramics is that it represents an *additive technology*. Clay is a more plastic medium than bone or stone; and therefore gave prehistoric

Head-Smashed-In Buffalo Jump is one of the oldest jumps in North America. The buffalo were stampeded along the drive lanes leading to the cliff's edge and the fatal plunge to their deaths. The animals were then butchered, the meat dried and the skins tanned.

DON INMAN '86

craftsmen more freedom over the final shape of a piece and more scope to express style. In *reductive technology*, such as stone tool-making, a mistake could not be easily undone. Since what is considered acceptable in style is conditioned by the aesthetic tastes of a cultural group, this additive technology has more potential to define prehistoric social units. Reductive technology has more limits due to the inherently less responsive nature of the material — there is less opportunity for style. (See Chapter 1.)

Although the pottery fragments uncovered from this time period are interesting, the Avonlea stone tools are more pleasing. Gifted craftsmen, the Avonlea flint-knappers produced some of the finest stone work ever seen in this province. The small arrowheads they crafted are thin, delicately shaped and symmetrical.

Were the Avonlea people as clever in hunting as the Besant? One of the most important Avonlea sites in Alberta, the Ramillies Pound north of Medicine Hat, suggests they were. Archaeologists have found butchered bones, bone tools and twenty-five Avonlea arrowheads. Prehistoric hunters could not have built a classic buffalo pound here because of the lack of wood; instead, they trapped bison by building a wall of earth and rock at the downslope end of a natural depression on the edge of a coulee — a clever innovation certainly in the same league as the Besant users' skillful hunt.

The Puzzle of Besant and Avonlea Coexistence

Archaeologists ask key questions about this period of time on the Alberta Plains. Why do Besant and Avonlea points occur simultaneously? Do the two styles of weapons indicate two ethnic groups, or a distinction within an ethnic group? If the apparent association of the points in some sites is correct, and the makers of the two styles camped together, then why are there two styles?

Reeves suggests that the superior social organization of Besant makers allowed them to expand at the expense of the Avonlea makers. Other archaeologists suggest that improved climatic conditions enabled both groups to find sustenance on the plains during this time. The question is far from being resolved.

SASKATCHEWAN BASIN
COMPLEX: Early Variant
(Avonlea Phase)

SASKATCHEWAN BASIN
COMPLEX: Late Variant
(Old Women's Phase)

CLUNY
COMPLEX
(One Gun Phase)

Wendy Johnson/ASA

Reconstructions of vessels representing the major prehistoric ceramic types found in Alberta.

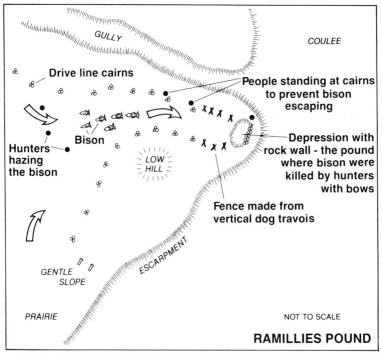

GULLY

COULEE

Drive line cairns

People standing at cairns
to prevent bison
escaping

Hunters
hazing
the bison

Bison

LOW
HILL

Depression with
rock wall - the pound
where bison were
killed by hunters
with bows

Fence made from
vertical dog travois

GENTLE
SLOPE

ESCARPMENT

PRAIRIE

NOT TO SCALE

RAMILLIES POUND

Wendy Johnson/ASA

Reconstruction of the bison kill at the Ramillies Pound site. The hunters drove the bison through a drive lane system to a rock-walled depression where the bison were trapped and killed.

(Next page) Plains camp. Alberta archaeologists believe the plains people lived in small mobile bands. They moved up to fifty times a year, either to trade with other bands, or to hunt buffalo.

The Old Women's Phase: Artists and Potters

The last prehistoric occupants of the plains, in the absence of tribal names, are said to belong to the *Old Women's Phase*. According to archaeologists, sites in a "phase" have common characteristics which likely indicate a cultural unit of some kind, although defining which kind may be difficult. They may, for example, be ethnic, tribal or political.

The Old Women's Phase is distinguished by a variety of small, side-notched points (arrowheads) which began to appear about 600 A.D. and continued to be produced until natives acquired European guns.

The term stems from Blackfoot mythology. According to a legend told by Natives to Hugh Dempsey, men and women once lived apart:

> Napi, a magician or "trickster," called the men together one day and suggested that both sexes live together. That way, the men could go hunting and to wars, while the women did the tanning and cooking. This sounded like a good idea to the men. So they went in search of the women and found them at the Women's Buffalo Jump, south of today's High River.
>
> The women's leader agreed to the plan, and it was decided that each woman would pick a man to be her partner.
>
> Crafty Napi, meanwhile, decided he wanted the most beautiful woman for himself. He dressed in women's clothing and stole back to the camp to decide which of the women was the fairest of them all.
>
> When it came time to pick partners, he was sorely disappointed. The beautiful woman he had chosen did not want him. Neither did the second most beautiful woman. When all the women had made their choices, Napi was the only one without a partner.
>
> Said Dempsey, in an interview recorded by Richard Forbis: "In anger, he went to the buffalo jump and changed himself into a pine tree. And there he stood alone, for many, many years."

Archaeologists deduce that the last prehistoric occupants of the plains were relatively stable and well adapted. This belief is based on the innumerable traces of their existence scattered over the windy plains: tipi rings, bison jumps, rock art and ceramics.

Who where they? Archaeologists think they see clues to this puzzle in the differences between arrowhead styles. The older

Blackfoot medicine men at Sun Dance Lodge.

The sandstone cliffs at Head-Smashed-In.

Excavating the Calderwood site near Head-Smashed-In.

Old Women's Phase arrowhead.

Mammoth tooth found near Edmonton.

arrowheads are more crudely shaped, leading to speculation that the early Old Women's Phase developed out of Besant, while the later, better-made examples may reflect Avonlea technology.

People from the Old Women's Phase were likely the major artists and craftsmen of the plains. Archaeologists think they were responsible for many of the red-ochre rock paintings and carvings which appear at dozens of sites in Alberta, such as Writing-On-Stone.

The people of the Old Women's Phase made extensive use of local stone such as small chert pebbles, but they also imported fine-quality stone from quarries in Wyoming, Montana, British Columbia and North Dakota. Their pottery became more complex, both in vessel form and decoration.

Archaeologists have also found more evidence of items of personal adornment from this time period. Prehistoric people fashioned beads into necklaces and other finery. The beads were made from cut and polished bone, stone and shell, as well as eagle talons and grizzly bear claws. These items may have held ceremonial significance.

The use of elk teeth sewn into dresses, rather like our sequins, is certain — archaeologists even find "fake" elk teeth made from carved bone. Porcupine quills were likely dyed and woven into geometric designs for trimming clothing.

Lumps of ochre are common in Old Women's campsites. The ochre, a natural iron compound, was ground up and applied as a red body paint.

Leisure in Prehistoric Times

From a twentieth century perspective, prehistoric life was grim. The lives of the last plains dwellers, however, may well have surpassed ours in at least one respect: leisure time. The mastery of bison-hunting may have left a great deal of opportunity for other activities. Dances, games and story-telling were immensely popular prehistoric activities.

We know little of how prehistoric people "managed" time. Studies of modern-day hunters and gatherers, however, yield some surprising facts. Men and women work an average of two or three hours a day to provide themselves with food. Another hour or two is devoted to food processing and preparation, the repair or manufacture of garments and tool and camp maintenance.

By our standards, the hunter-gatherer's way of life leaves a considerable amount of leisure time for visiting and resting. There is no reason to assume prehistoric people were much different.

Something New on the Plains

The plains, by the beginning of the eighteenth century, stood at the precipitous edge of change. A vast, technological society devoted to possessions, to status, and to territory, waited in the wings.

Anthony Henday, the first white person to penetrate central and southern Alberta, would not arrive until 1754-55. Horses, however, would appear by 1730, traded and stolen from tribes in the central and southern plains. Their presence fundamentally changed the buffalo hunt and with it the basis of 10,000 years of plains life. Other trade goods such as guns, axes, knives and cookwares, especially copper kettles, would begin to transform prehistoric life long before a white face appeared.

One startling archaeological find stands at the dawn of Alberta history. The Cluny site, at Blackfoot Crossing on the Bow River (about 110 kilometres east of the junction of the Bow and Elbow Rivers where Calgary stands today), is where a mysterious group of outsiders built a fortified earthlodge village and lived for perhaps a few months sometime between 1730 and 1750.

The village they constructed was unlike anything ever seen in Alberta. It consisted of a semi-circular ditch terminating at a terrace edge. The ditch was bridged by at least three causeways with a palisade constructed parallel to the ditch. Eleven large pits, whose function is unclear, are situated between the ditch and the palisade.

The style of village is similar to that which existed around the same time along the Missouri River in North and South Dakota. There, occupants planted corn in plots along the river and lived in semi-subterranean earthlodges enclosed within fortified villages.

Archaeologists are just as intrigued by the distinctive pottery fragments found at Cluny as they are by its architecture. These fragments sometimes feature a brushed surface,

R.G. Forbis conducting Medicine Wheel research.

Measuring location of an artifact.

(Opposite page) Colin Robertson of the Hudson's Bay Company trading goods for pelts with the Natives.

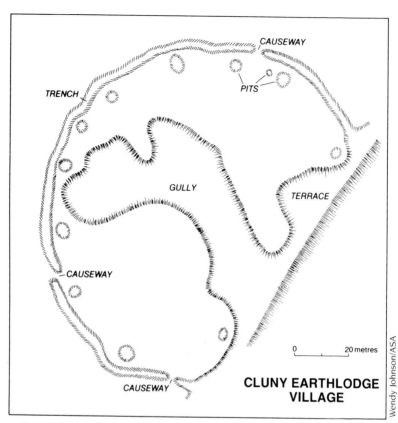

CAUSEWAY

TRENCH

PITS

GULLY

TERRACE

CAUSEWAY

0   20 metres

CAUSEWAY

**CLUNY EARTHLODGE
VILLAGE**

Cluny Earthlodge Village, reminiscent of Middle Missouri Villages found in the midwestern United States.

showing small lines created by the bristles. Some display "grooved paddle impressions." Flat wooden paddles were used to imprint parallel or criss-cross grooves. Unusual "knotted cord" impressions are also common. These appear as though someone took a string, tied knots closely together, then pushed the string into the surface thereby creating dimples and grooves.

Yet another unusual characteristic is the use of a dentate stamp, rare in other examples of Saskatchewan River basin ceramics. Toothed objects were also pushed into the vessel. These appear in regular intervals usually near the rim and serve as a decoration. Lastly, Cluny potters fashioned collared or "braced" rims, thickened for several centimetres from the top.

Pottery of this kind is also found in small quantities along the Red Deer, Bow and Oldman River (but not along the Milk River in the south). Archaeologists refer to the ceramics found at these sites and at Cluny as the *One Gun Phase.*

The One Gun Phase, of which the Cluny site is the prime example, represents an actual migration of people from the Middle Missouri area of North Dakota, concluded W. J. Byrne, now Assistant Deputy Minister for the Historical Resources Division of Alberta Culture.

These people may have attempted to grow corn, but it seems apparent from their relatively short stay, that whatever way of life they attempted was unsuccessful. In all likelihood, they abandoned the Cluny village within a year.

Perhaps the Cluny dwellers turned to bison-hunting, an exciting proposition now that the horse and gun had arrived. According to this theory, the men and their wives dispersed into Native populations and continued to make their distinctive pottery. The sites where their ceramics have been found show former Cluny residents probably stayed in the south-central part of the province and did not progress as far north as the North Saskatchewan River.

Were the Cluny residents escaping disease, or other tribes displaced westward by Europeans? Were they part of a chain reaction driving Native groups further west as Europeans advanced? These are among the host of unanswered questions surrounding the enigmatic Cluny dwellers.

"Whatever became of them, the remnants of the ancient fortification at Cluny bear mute testimony to a courageous and industrious people of pioneering blood," wrote Richard Forbis in *Cluny, An Ancient Fortified Village in Alberta.*

Time, as the Cluny site reveals, was running out for the traditional way of life on the plains. Had the Cluny people arrived in Alberta only a few decades later, European observers may have revealed more about them in historic records.

The Blackfoot: Recent Arrivals on the Plains?

A puzzle perplexing both scholars and the public is the tribal identity of prehistoric bands. The descriptions given by early fur traders are rather confusing. In August, 1754, Henday described meeting "Archithinue" Indians. Did he mean

Ribstone found near Viking.

Example of pictograph found at Spray Canyon.

(Opposite page) Alberta's first artists left hundreds of individual petroglyphs on the soft sandstone cliffs of Writing-On-Stone.

Blackfoot, as the editor of his journal suggested? Or non-Cree, because "Ayatchiyinwiw" is the Cree word for stranger?

The fact that horses and guns arrived on the plains before Europeans adds immeasurably to the tangle. These innovations led to the shifting of Native populations before explorers and fur traders were able to record what they observed. The Blackfoot, for example, may have been recent arrivals to Alberta's Plains.

We do know that when the first Europeans arrived on the plains of Alberta and Saskatchewan, they found a vibrant mix of Native tribes. These included the Blackfoot, Blood, Piegan, Sarsi, portions of Assiniboine, the Snake and the Gros Ventres.

Around 1700, the section of northern Alberta north of the Saskatchewan River appears to have been occupied by the Athapaskan-speaking Beaver, Slavey and Chipewyan. The Blackfoot Confederacy (composed of three distinct tribes; the Peigan, Blood and the Blackfoot Proper) occupied central Alberta between Red Deer and Calgary, and the Snake roamed out of Montana as far north as Calgary.

The Kutenai, meanwhile, inhabited the southwestern mountains and foothills of Alberta. To the east, the Cree occupied the forests of northern Saskatchewan and Manitoba to Hudson Bay. The Gros Ventres and the Assiniboine inhabited the southern plains of Saskatchewan and Manitoba.

Most observers believe that, with the introduction of guns, tribes began to move south or southwesterly in the mid or late eighteenth century. The Snake, stricken with disease, shifted south into Montana. The Blackfoot moved south to fill much of the plains proper, as far south as the Sweetgrass Hills. The Sarsi became firmly established in the Bow Valley, but moved with Blackfoot groups.

To the north, the Cree, armed with guns, displaced the Beaver in the Athabasca Valley prior to 1760. In turn, the Beaver spread east, pushing the Sekani towards the Rocky Mountains.

None of these changes have been demonstrated in the archaeological record. Indeed, some archaeologists seriously question whether stone tools are sensitive indicators of culture. Jack Brink dismisses as wishful thinking the Hollywood stereotype of a cowboy pulling the arrow from the side of a covered wagon and coolly announcing "Comanche." Other

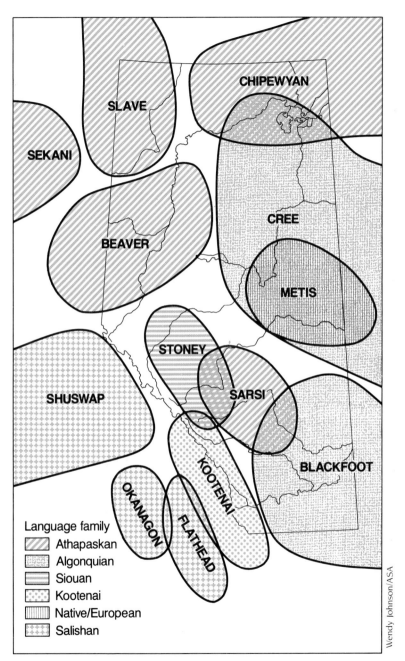

Language family

- ▨ Athapaskan
- ▦ Algonquian
- ▤ Siouan
- ▩ Kootenai
- ▥ Native/European
- ▦ Salishan

Distribution of Native Indian groups in Alberta and neighbouring areas in the early historic period, about A.D. 1850.

Wendy Johnson/ASA

117

Fort Dunvegan in the Peace River district was occupied by both traders and missionaries from 1805 to 1918.

archaeologists are intrigued by remarks like those of Henry Kelsey, who in 1691, suggested that the Assiniboine could discriminate their arrows from those of others, such as the Blackfoot.

Tribal affiliations on the prehistoric plains, it appears, will remain an enigma until archaeological research in this area can be refined. Even with that refinement, complex problems will likely remain.

"It is very possible that the concept of territory, as we think of it, was lacking among prehistoric Plains Indians and only exists in the records as a European imposition," says Brink.

Henday, Horses and Guns

The archaeological record is relatively sparse for the time span called the *Protohistoric*, which began with the arrival of the horse and gun and lasted until the North West Mounted Police arrived in 1874.

Historic records tell us that Henday arrived in the autumn of 1754 with a clear mandate: to determine whether the Natives could be convinced to hunt and trap for his employer, the Hudson's Bay Company.

Although the Natives he met along the way had never before seen a white face, they had already acquired some of the tools of European civilization through Cree middlemen in the fur trade. For decades, these middlemen ran a profitable business by purchasing furs from Natives in Saskatchewan and Alberta, and transporting them hundreds of kilometres back to York Factory on Hudson Bay.

When French traders from Montreal began to build trading posts inland, the Hudson's Bay Company found its profits seriously threatened. Company officials sent Henday into Alberta to explore ways to counter this serious rivalry.

As Henday explored central and southern Alberta, the paying guest of a Cree band, he could not have known that this territory — later to become Alberta — represented one of North America's last pockets of prehistoric life.

"The time had come when Alberta's Indians, instead of merely feeling the effects of white man's goods, were soon to see trading posts erected in their midst," wrote James G. MacGregor in *A History of Alberta*.

Henday personified the pressures of civilization which were

slowly beginning to filter into Alberta from three directions: the east, the west and the south. Only parts of present-day Alaska, the Northwest Territories, the Yukon and northern British Columbia would escape European civilization longer than Alberta.

One day in mid-October, journeying on or near the Red Deer River near present-day Drumheller, Henday's party came across a large Native camp of more than 200 tipis and perhaps 1,600 persons.

Would they agree to become hunters and trappers for the northern fur trade? The Natives declined. Fur resources were scant on the plains, so they would have to strike into the northern forests to trap furs. To receive any goods for their furs, they would have to exchange their beloved horses for canoes and make an arduous five or six-week trip to York Factory.

According to Henday's journals, the chief explained these reasons for not taking up the fur trade. Then he added another, even more compelling argument:

> The chief further said they never wanted food, as they followed the buffalo and killed them with bows and arrows; and he was informed the natives that frequented the settlements were oftentimes starved on their journey. Such remarks I thought exceedingly true.

The Florescence of the Plains Way of Life

Archaeologists and historians speak of the period between 1750 and 1850 as the *florescence* or flowering of the Plains Indians way of life. Aided in the hunt by horses, Natives escalated the bison hunt to a level never to be seen again. They also acquired more leisure time which they devoted to decorative arts, to religious societies and to warfare. Historians note that the easier availability of food allowed the formation of larger bands, which in turn contributed to a stronger sense of solidarity among the entire Blackfoot Confederacy.

The absence of prime fur-bearing animals on the plains kept the fur-trading companies from building forts in the south. Instead, traders built several forts and posts along the North Saskatchewan River, at places like Rocky Mountain House, Edmonton House and Fort George.

"In this way, the daily lives of the Plains Indians were not

Kootenay Plains Sun Dance Lodge.

Excavation of a tipi ring.

Jack Ives/ASA

Survey for Beaver River Sandstone, MacKay River.

ASA

Excavation of a Boreal Forest site.

directly affected like those in the north who were encouraged to become trappers and hunters for the trading companies," noted Hugh Dempsey in *Indian Tribes of Alberta.*

Impact of the "Big Dogs"

The introduction of the horse, far more than guns, fundamentally changed the way of life on the plains during the Protohistoric. The changes, of course, did not happen all at once. From later historical records, it is estimated that horses were present in the Bow Valley by 1730. By 1745, when Henday travelled in central and south Alberta, horses appear to have been well-established.

David Thompson's storyteller, an old Cree named Saukamappee, recounted that his enemies and their allies "had Misstutin (Big Dogs, that is, horses) on which they rode, swift as the deer, on which they dashed at the Peeagans, and with their stone Pukamoggan (clubs) knocking them on the head."

The archaeological record has not yet revealed much information about the impact of the horse on plains society. Historical evidence, however, reveals that the horse did far more than make bison-hunting easier; it changed the entire strategy of the hunt. Bands no longer walked two or three days to a good site for a communal hunt. On a horse, a bison herd would rarely be more than an hour away.

This allowed far more freedom. Rather than planning every detail of a hunt, they could be more casual. If Natives on horseback failed to kill any bison, it would probably not take them long to find another herd. Aided by the horse and gun, Plains Indians adapted some of their previous techniques, such as the bison jump and simple surround, but they were able to kill many more animals. The gun did not, however, completely replace the bow and arrow for the hunt. In many cases it remained easier to use the bow and arrow than the often-unreliable guns.

The horse changed other time-consuming aspects of the hunt. Previously, the whole camp might travel after a kill to a large butchering site to process the meat. It was then transported by dog-pulled travois, a method that rarely allowed camps to move more than twenty kilometres a day.

With the arrival of the horse, meat from butchered animals could easily be loaded on horseback and transported quickly to a distant camp.

Equally significant, the horse made it possible for Natives to hunt bison individually with a degree of safety previously unknown. Suddenly it was not only possible, but practical, for an individual to go out and kill enough bison for his family's needs.

Two other changes occurred simultaneously. First, the horse altered people's sense of property. Previously, few opportunities presented themselves for individuals to acquire individual wealth. Horses, which represented hunting power, now became an accepted sign of wealth. There are accounts of Blackfoot warriors who owned as many as 100 horses; to steal a horse from another tribe became an ultimate test of bravery.

Second, a new sense of territory and tribalism also seems to have appeared. Warfare, which probably always existed, became more fierce with the horse and the gun. Different bands raided and battled to maintain or extend their hunting territories. The Blackfoot, in particular, became known as the fierce lords of the plains. They waged bloody battles with the Snake, eventually beating them south into Montana.

Blackfoot camp with horse travois, 1883.

(Next page) Life in the Northern Forest required special skills and inventiveness to match the demands of the environment.

By the early 1800s, the Blackfoot controlled the vast area between the North Saskatchewan on the north, the Missouri River on the south and the Saskatchewan border on the east.

David Thompson's informant, Saukamappee, who spent most of his life with the Blackfoot, describes the first use of guns against the Snake sometime between 1700 and 1725: "We watched our opportunity when they drew their arrows to shoot at us, their bodies were then exposed and each of us, as opportunity offered, fired with deadly aim and either killed or severely wounded, everyone we aimed at."

Fur Trade, Smallpox and the Decline of the Bison

Unlike their northern counterparts, Plains Natives did not actively engage in fur-trading until after 1832, when the first steamboat chugged up the Missouri as far as Fort Union, near present-day Williston, Montana. This created a way for American traders to purchase and ship buffalo robes and hides from the Natives to markets in the East. (The bulkiness of these goods prevented the Hudson's Bay Company from engaging in the robe trade.)

A threat as lethal to Plains Indians as guns and alcohol showed its deadly face by 1781 — smallpox. Almost two-thirds of the Blackfoot Nation (6,000 individuals) are believed to have died in a second epidemic in 1837, brought in by American fur traders. Trader Alexander Cuthbertson recounted finding only two debilitated women survivors in a Piegan camp of sixty lodges.

Following this last pestilence, the Blackfoot faced yet another challenge to their existence: declining bison herds. In September, 1845, when artist Paul Kane rode from Fort Carlton to Edmonton, he noted:

> During the whole of three days it took us to reach Edmonton House, we saw nothing else but these animals covering the Plains as far as the eye could reach, and so numerous were they, that at times they impeded our progress, filling the air with dust almost to suffocation. We killed whenever we required a supply of food, selecting the fattest of the cows, taking only the tongue and boss, or hump, for our present meal, and not burdening ourselves unnecessarily with more.

It became clear by 1857, when the British and Canadian governments sent Capt. John Palliser to study the prairies, that bison populations were seriously diminished. One member of the expedition, Lt. Thomas Blakiston, noted that the Natives "are aware that the buffalo are rapidly decreasing, and foresee that their descendants will have to take to some other way of living. . ."

That time was not far away. In 1869, the Canadian government purchased all Hudson's Bay Company lands, including Alberta. With the establishment of the first North West Mounted Police post in Alberta, at Fort Macleod in 1874, the way opened for settlers and ranchers to begin trickling in.

Little remained of the great herds of bison which had populated the plains for so many millenia. It is estimated that the buffalo population in North America totalled roughly 60 million in 1790; by 1890, official records put the remaining number at 1,090.

For Chief Sweetgrass of the Plains Cree, the scarcity of bison meant that "our country is no longer able to support us." By 1871, he and other chiefs were appealing for a government treaty to save at least some of their former hunting territory.

In 1877, Chief Crowfoot led the Blackfoot Confederacy to accept Treaty Seven thereby giving up their rights to almost a third of the province south of the Red Deer River. Prior to signing the treaty, he stated:

> . . . I have to speak for my people. . . The plains are large and wide; we are the children of the plains; this has long been our home and the buffalo have long been our food.
>
> If the police had not come to this country, where would we all be now? Bad men and whisky were killing us so fast that very few of us would have been alive today. The Mounted Police have protected us as the feathers of the bird protect it from the frosts of winter. I wish all my people good and trust that all our hearts will increase in goodness from this time forward. I am satisfied. I will sign the treaty.

The Drive Lanes of Deception

Long before Stonehenge appeared on England's Salisbury Plain, hunters in Alberta began building an intricate network of rocks that displayed similar prehistoric ingenuity.

Today, these small rock cairns barely poke above the prairie grasses at Head-Smashed-In Buffalo Jump. Over the last 5,500 years, the cairns played a vital role in gathering bison to the kill site below the cliff.

The drive lanes were used at almost all bison jumps. They consist of rock piles placed five to ten metres apart, which prehistoric people heaped high with piles of buffalo chips, sod and brush.

The cairns were strategically placed to confine the stampeding animals within the exact areas which would lead to the kill area. Expert buffalo runners were dispatched to coax the bison inside the lanes.

The geography of Head-Smashed-In made proper placement of the cairns more vital than at other bison jumps. Drives at classic jumps form a V-shaped funnel, with the wide end extending to the area where the animals were gathered and the narrow end stopping at the cliff's edge.

The rolling, hilly country at Head-Smashed-In

The drive lanes consisted of rock piles, buffalo chips and brush.

requires a much more sophisticated drive lane system to effectively channel herds. Lanes were built not only to direct bison to the jump site, but also to keep them from veering over the wrong ridge or into a tributary valley. One wrong turn could ruin the hunt and cut sharply into the winter food supplies for several bands.

The system of drive lanes at Head-Smashed-In is the largest and most elaborate of any known buffalo jump in North America. It consists of thousands of individual cairns and dozens of drive lanes. Some extend as far away as ten kilometres from the cliff site. Many generations of prehistoric people likely laboured over the gradual improvement of the system.

Time is needed to understand the story written in the bones and stones of the Porcupine Hills. Admittedly, the impact of Head-Smashed-In is more subtle than that of Stonehenge.

Head-Smashed-In shares a "world heritage" designation with Stonehenge, an honour awarded to approximately 150 outstanding sites in the world. The importance of Head-Smashed-In was further recognized by the opening of a ten-million dollar interpretive centre, open year-round, in the summer of 1987.

Buffalo: One Stop Shopping

Bison have been called the "walking supermarket" of the plains, and with good reason.

Just as the mega-stores of today can meet almost all the consumers' needs, the great buffalo herds once supplied Natives with everything from housing to cutlery.

Prehistoric people fashioned bison bones into tools such as needles and awls for perforating leather. Horns were made into spoons and containers; hooves had a second-life as rattles. Fresh blood and marrow from the bones were regarded as tasty snacks.

Tipis consisted of buffalo hides draped over woo-

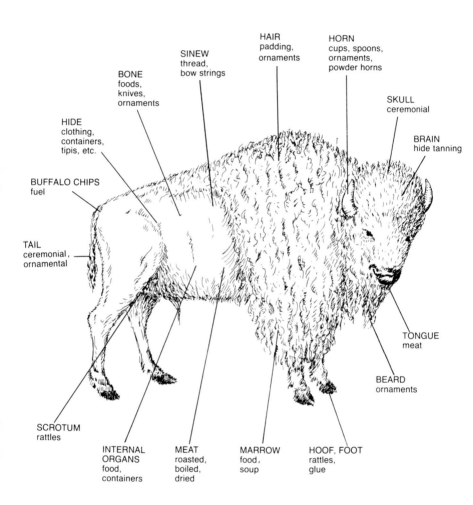

HAIR
padding,
ornaments

HORN
cups, spoons,
ornaments,
powder horns

SINEW
thread,
bow strings

BONE
foods,
knives,
ornaments

SKULL
ceremonial

BRAIN
hide tanning

HIDE
clothing,
containers,
tipis, etc.

BUFFALO CHIPS
fuel

TAIL
ceremonial,
ornamental

TONGUE
meat

BEARD
ornaments

SCROTUM
rattles

INTERNAL
ORGANS
food,
containers

MEAT
roasted,
boiled,
dried

MARROW
food,
soup

HOOF, FOOT
rattles,
glue

The Bison Supermarket of the Plains

Ewa Pluciennik

den frameworks for shelter. Each tipi required ten to fifteen hides and needed to be replaced every few years. Hides were too thick to be used for clothing, but served as shields, robes and blankets. Tails and skulls were sometimes used in religious ceremonies.

Although most bison parts were likely used in difficult times, prehistoric people were not always so prudent. There is evidence hunters sometimes became frenzied during bison hunts and killed far more animals than they needed.

Sometimes they only took the tongue and left the rest of the carcass to rot. Records show more than 1,000 bison were sometimes killed at once. No doubt huge numbers of carcasses must have been wasted.

Prehistoric people left evidence of both prudent and wasteful attitudes to natural resources.

The Mystery of Nelson Small Legs

What of modern-day use of vision sites? The Head-Smashed-In site provides one tantalizing clue. On the hilltop near the vision quest structure, small stones have been used to spell out the words: "Nelson Small Legs." Small Legs Jr. was the southern Alberta director of the American Indian Movement. The son of a chief, he killed himself on May 16, 1976, on the Piegan Reserve in southern Alberta to protest federal treatment of his people.

"If vision quest sites can serve a memorial function in modern times, then it is possible that they may have served similar purposes in the past," noted Christopher Hughes, who wrote of the phenomenon while in the University of Alberta's Anthropology Department.

Did Small Legs himself leave the memorial? Or, more likely, was it built in his memory? The discovery adds one more dimension to what appears to be a fascinating revitalization of vision-questing among today's Natives.

The Vision Seekers

Buffalo were perhaps not the only reason why young men climbed the grassy hills above Head-Smashed-In. They may have journeyed there to seek visions.

A spot just north of the buffalo jump near Fort Macleod has been identified as a *vision quest* site. It consists of a small stone structure and several smaller clusters of stone. The stone structure is oval in shape and is oriented on an east-west axis, a distinguishing feature of most vision quest sites.

The site is one of many officially-reported vision quest sites in Alberta. Others have been found in such places as Dinosaur Provincial Park, Limestone Mountain overlooking the Clearwater River Valley in southwestern Alberta and in Waterton Lakes National Park.

Some sites are still used. When a forest lookout ranger came across one such site on an exposed ridge on Limestone Mountain in 1984, he found fairly recent offerings of meat.

Usually vision quest sites are situated in a place with a marvelous view across the plains or mountain ranges. They tend to be on an east-west axis, which may spring from a belief that nothing must come between the supplicant and the Northern Star which is believed to hold supernatural powers. Or they could be aligned to the rising and setting of the sun.

Archaeologists believe ancient people used such sites to seek prowess from supernatural forces. No one knows when the ritual of vision-questing began, although it appears to be part of ancient shamanistic traditions which may trace their roots back 20,000 or 30,000 years.

We know from historic accounts that vision-questing amounted to a rite of passage into manhood. A young man would bring offerings such as eagle feathers or cloths to the site. He would then enter a "fasting structure" perhaps a metre in height and constructed of hides or sandstone slabs.

John Cooper, in *The Gros Ventres of Montana*,

describes the vision quest of an Indian called Little Man:

"Little Man had (during a vision quest event) a little oblong nest with rocks piled up about two or three feet high, and open toward his feet. This is called his 'call-for-power lodge.' "

The young man would then fast, likely in solitude, for several days, hoping a vision would appear to him. He would usually enter a trance-like state. At some point a magical animal might befriend him, teach him how such an animal behaves and give him special instructions designed to increase his "personal power" as a hunter.

Today, some anthropologists believe that vision quests, divination and other appeals to the supernatural may have had pragmatic value in prehistoric societies.

Robin Ridington, in *Northern Hunting Technology*, argues that such beliefs encourage hunters to gain the kind of knowledge they need to survive. Careful study of animal behaviour, for example, would be invaluable to the hunter.

"Personal knowledge as a source of power is of practical and symbolic importance in very many hunting and gathering societies," writes Ridington.

Alberta's First Artists

The stark figure of a tall person holding a hoop in one hand is painted on the limestone walls of the Spray Canyon near Canmore.

The figure may have been there before the building of Carthage or the capture of Nineveh. If civilization is kind, it will be there when most of the art of our time is faded and forgotten. No one knows the identity of the prehistoric Picassos who etched their timeless rock art into the Alberta landscape over thousands of years.

Rock art is divided into two types. *Pictographs* are paintings executed on rock with a mixture of red ochre, animal grease and water, whereas *petroglyphs*, are figures cut or etched into rock.

Prehistoric artists painted people in a variety of ways. Sometimes they drew them in movement, sometimes as warriors carrying round shields or as simple stick figures. Animals also enliven the rock walls. Bison, bears, dogs, horses, snakes, birds, animal tracks and many unidentified beasts frequently appear.

Of the several dozen rock art sites identified in Alberta, most have been found in the southwest. The province contains one of the largest and most awesome rock art sites in Western North America at Writing-On-Stone Provincial Park in south-central Alberta. Only one possible rock art site has yet been found in northern Alberta, near Fort McMurray. There may be others which have so far escaped discovery.

Most rock art appears on sheltered rock walls, some in caves or shelters. Hundreds of individual petroglyphs are etched into the soft sandstone cliffs of Writing-On-Stone.

Unfortunately, the age of most rock art cannot be accurately determined. Archaeologists suspect that the majority was produced within the last thousand years. Depictions of European trade goods such as guns and horses clearly show that rock art continued into the historic period.

Some archaeologists believe that differences in style may indicate different groups of people. In Alberta, for example, fish motifs appear only on rock art in the Rockies, although they are common in British Columbia. Does this suggest a connection between the Rocky mountains and the interior of British Columbia?

Were prehistoric people just doodling? This seems unlikely, although the true purpose of rock art is unclear. Rock art may have played a part in ceremonial or religious observances. We know from historic accounts that some rock art sites were used for vision quests, and that Natives looked upon Writing-On-Stone as a sacred place where spirits wrote on stone.

Of Writing-On-Stone, Hugh Dempsey once wrote:

"Because of the power of the pictographs the Blackfeet were afraid to stay there overnight. 'In earlier
days the Piegans camped in the Milk River Valley
but never camped close to Writing-On-Stone,' said
Yellow Kidney. 'Groups visited it at times to see the
writings. People feared it.'"

Tipis — The Portable Plains Home

The tipi or lodge of the Plains Indian is one of the
most sophisticated dwellings ever developed. The
elegant high roofline and the smoke flaps allowed a
fire to be burned within, while an inner liner
prevented drafts, providing both an aesthetic and
utilitarian solution to survival in a harsh, often treeless environment.

In ancient times, the tipi's bottom edge was held
down by rocks. These rocks formed circles of stone
which can still be seen in southern Alberta. They
are called tipi rings and mark the location of former
campsites.

Historic tribes such as the Blackfoot rigidly struc-
tured their use of space within the tipi. Some areas
were set apart for sleeping, some for ceremonial
purposes, and some for cooking. Archaeologists try
to find evidence for such spatial patterns in ancient
tipi rings.

Changes in the conception and use of space may
provide clues for discovering different peoples in
the past. This difficult task is an on-going research
topic for Alberta archaeologists.

Jim Burns excavating a 10,000-year-old elk near Watino.

5

Prehistoric Life in the Northern Forests

The time is an early winter morning many hundreds of years ago. Above an ice-covered lake, two small mooseskin lodges stand in a clearing among the spruce trees. Last night's snowfall has covered the footprints around the camp, making the brown lodges look somewhat like huge fungi springing from the forest floor. Only thin columns of smoke from the lodges betray human presence.

Two young men dressed in furs emerge from separate shelters. They reach back inside and withdraw wooden spears tipped with sharp, carefully-fashioned stone points.

The hunters then turn to take another tool still in use today and largely unchanged. They attach the snowshoes, made from sinew and supple birch branches, to their moccasins with hide straps and now float easily over the powdery snow into the mossy forest. The big animals they seek — the moose, the wood buffalo, the caribou — sink deeply in the soft snow. The forest dwellers have an advantage, thanks to their wits.

The two men are brothers, married to two sisters from another family. A third brother remains in his lodge covered with furs up to the neck. He is feeling too sick to hunt today. He is with his wife (who is another sister), and her father. The father is widowed and too old to join in the hunt.

The sun strikes the little clearing, although it is too weak to warm the air. Three women, wearing lighter furs than their husbands, walk down to the lake. They do not have snowshoes, so they have to wade through the soft snow as they head across the ice to check their fishing nets. They find they have caught three medium-sized whitefish.

The older children go into the woods to inspect snares for snowshoe hares, and return happily with four in hand. Tonight, the small group will dine well on fish and hare, chewed with a bit of dried moose meat.

Don Inman

Camp life in the Northern Forest.

This routine, more or less, continues all month with almost equal success. Despite the help the snowshoes give the hunters in deep snow, the men have been unable to approach any big game. Meanwhile, the weather is turning colder and the daylight hunting hours shorter. Finally, the men return jubilantly to camp. Food! They have managed to kill two buffalo in deep snow. Firewood is becoming scarce by the lake camp so the group decides to move camp inland to the kill site, carrying hot coals, their lodgeskins and a few possessions.

Inland, the meat is butchered and the remains frozen for later use. For the rest of the winter, these forest people catch small game — mostly hares, sometimes a few fish. Occasionally, the hunters take a moose or some woodland caribou.

Although the snow is receding and travel is easier, the game becomes even scarcer. The group decides to split up, some try fishing upriver, others join relatives downriver where they believe moose have now moved. In the clearing by the lake, only the lodge poles remain, to stand like sentinels over the silent camp.

Life in the North: Predictably Unpredictable

This seems almost like a dream today because archaeologists do not know as much about prehistoric forest people as they do about prehistoric plains people. Accounts of life in the northern forests are largely conjecture.

Even today, the forested northern half of the province remains sparsely populated, even mysterious. Travel Alberta tourist brochures describe the area as "a vast land of rugged forests, teeming lakes and untamed rivers." Fishermen pay high prices to charter floatplanes for flights into some remote northern lakes; satellite transmissions bring television reception to its far-flung communities. Yet, in many ways, the isolation and challenge presented by the boreal forest is unchanged from prehistoric times.

Ewa Pluciennik

Snowshoe hare.

Some who live there today would perhaps share the feelings of their ancestors of up to 10,000 years ago, who doubtless found the terrain cold and hard. The forest, however, is also beautiful in its vastness, and abundant enough for those humans who understand the underlying dynamics of boreal forest ecology, rhythms that are predictably unpredictable.

Moose

Ewa Pluciennik

In prehistoric times, as now, game that flourished one year might be scarce the next. Records of fur-trading posts across northern Canada, for example, show the population of snowshoe hares cycled from a high of 90,000 to less than 10,000 and then back to a high of 150,000 between 1855 and 1865. This cycle is repeated every nine to ten years and affects many other animals, including the chief predator of the hare, the lynx. (In turn, lynx become desperate when hares disappear, and may seek less characteristic prey like caribou calves.)

Although plains people relied on the bison for almost all their needs, the forest dwellers were not so fortunate. They had no one dependable source of sustenance. From a hilltop, plains dwellers could see buffalo from a distance of many kilometres. In the thick undulating forest, big game had to be tracked and then stalked, an uncertain pursuit.

Even when hunters succeeded in killing a moose, the chances were remote that another would be nearby. Moose, unlike bison, are solitary animals; woodland caribou roam in small groups. No large herds could be captured in the forest, therefore, many hunts were doomed to failure.

As though cold temperatures, huge territory and fluctuating game were not enough, forest dwellers had to contend with deep, soft snow, unlike the hard-packed snowcrust or land drifted bare often found on the plains.

Although life in the northern forest could be harsh, the people possessed the knowledge to persist for 10,000 years. The early Albertans learned to weave willow for fishing, they fashioned snowgoggles to protect their eyes from glare and, they developed such efficient ways to walk on snow that they may have been able to outrun caribou under some conditions. They appear to have possessed a kinship system so sophisticated they could identify hundreds of their relatives over great distances.

Alberta's Northern Archaeological Puzzle

The thick forest does not easily yield the secrets of the past. Alberta archaeologists know from Paleo-Indian finds in Peace River Country and from Agate Basin specimens at the Beaver River Quarry near Fort MacKay in northeastern Alberta that people occupied the province's northern forests as far back as 10,000 to 8,000 years ago. Yet no one is certain they remained in the forest, or merely journeyed there occasionally to hunt and fish. At Wentzel Lake, north of the present-day community of Fort Vermilion, fragments of stone tools and charcoal have been found, indicating a campsite which has been dated by the radiocarbon method to 5,200 years ago.

The discovery of two distinctive types of projectile points, McKean and Oxbow, along the southern edge of the boreal forest fuels speculation that plains people may have expanded north into the aspen parklands edging the boreal forest 4,000 to 5,000 years ago. By 2,500 years ago, projectile points found in the boreal forest of Alberta bear more similarity with those of the Taltheilei tradition of the Northwest Territories than with those found on the plains, thinks Jack Ives.

Excavations at the Duckett site, near Cold Lake in northeastern Alberta, have revealed archaeological evidence of human presence in the district for possibly the last 10,000 years. This site is situated near the southern fringe of the boreal forest. Shifts in the position of the forest during the prehistoric past have some interesting implications for the archaeological record of Duckett.

Gloria Fedirchuk and Ed McCullough, the archaeologists who excavated the site, noted:

> . . . we are left with the difficulty that the southern edge of the lake district in which the Duckett site is situated lies in an area close enough to the plains that past fluctuations in the boreal forest could have brought Plains bison hunters northwards, or forest-adapted populations using stemmed points southward.

Little is known about life in northern Alberta before the fur traders. In part, this is due to slightly acidic soils in the boreal forest that quickly destroy wood and hasten the decomposition of bone.

This leaves an archaeological record composed mainly of only the most durable items: stone tools and by-products from their manufacture. Unlike the plains, where literally boxcars of bones and artifacts have been found at single sites, such great abundance or diversity of tools has yet to be unearthed in those jumbled woods.

Reconstructed clay pot fragment from Black Fox Island.

Courtesy Kathy Connor-Learn/ASA

Excavating the Duckett site.

Soil, moreover, accumulates so gradually on most northern forest sites that a mere twenty centimetres of earth may represent 10,000 years of the past. Finally, there are cultural reasons for such scant evidence. Boreal forest peoples typically lived in small groups, which moved frequently. Their legacy was not left in the form of pyramids or temples.

Since traditional archaeology has so far yielded only faint clues about the life of northern forest dwellers, archaeologists must look in other directions. The search will involve looking to Natives, for whom Alberta's prehistoric past is a living legacy; to the environment, which leaves natural clues embedded in soil, pollen, rock and wood; and, to their own powers of close observation and analysis.

From Ice Age to Forest

This much is clear: life in the forest was in sharp contrast to that of the plains and parklands.

Alberta's boreal forest, as we know it, has existed only for almost 4,000 years. During the last glaciation, ice more than a kilometre high covered all of northern Alberta. Unlike the southern plains and parts of the province associated with the ice-free corridor, this huge area could not have been occupied by humans until the ice sheets began to retreat between 12,000 and 13,000 years ago.

The first boreal forest, composed of spruce, probably spread northwards from the United States at the end of the last glaciation. The first trees may even have taken root in layers of sediment deposited over the remaining northern ice. Remains of bison, horses, camels, elk and woolly mammoths have been unearthed from this period in the Peace River district.

In southern Alberta, this spruce forest appears to have lasted until about 10,000 years ago. Afterwards, it was replaced by grassland which pushed further north than it is today. The spruce forest predominated in the north until about 8,000 years ago, by which time all remnants of ice sheets had disappeared. Moose, woodland caribou and bison ranged throughout.

By then, species like pine and birch began to migrate northward. These species mixed with spruce and aspen to create a forest environment. The modern boreal forest was in place around 4,000 years ago, at a time of slightly cooler, wetter weather.

It was the same kind of forest everywhere. The boreal zone, a broad belt of coniferous-dominated forest across North America, Asia and Europe, differs relatively little, whether in Alaska, Newfoundland, Alberta or Eurasia. Such a landscape is characterized by its patchiness. It is a world of thick woods, moss and muskeg, many small lakes and ponds, interspersed with open knolls of aspen and pine.

Today, Alberta's northern forests are home to moose, woodland caribou, deer, timber wolf, coyote, lynx, black bear, beaver, muskrat, porcupine and hare, among others. All these animals likely inhabited the northern forest for thousands of years; wood bison were common until late in the last century.

Identifying the Forest Dwellers

In the absence of definitive evidence, scientists speculate that prehistoric people may have entered the boreal forest in essentially three ways. People from the plains may have followed bison herds into the forest and parklands during the warm period after the glaciers. Some bison undoubtedly sought winter shelter along the southern edge of the forest.

Excavation of a Boreal Forest site.

Skull of a 10,000-year-old elk found near Watino.

As well, Arctic hunters from what is now the Northwest Territories may have followed barren-ground caribou into the boreal forest. These caribou migrate from summer range on the tundra to winter range in the forest. The seasonal movements of bison and caribou may have brought hunters into the forest, after which long-term adaptations to this environment may have occurred. Finally, people already adapted to life in the boreal forests of Alaska and the Yukon may have expanded to the south and west.

Ewa Pluciennik

Bobcat

By 2,500 years ago, ties between boreal forest dwellers and peoples of the forests and treeline areas to the north appear to have been stronger than with the plains people.

Although so much of forest settlement remains a mystery, Alberta archaeologists believe it is reasonable to assume that Beaver Indians occupied much of northern Alberta between the Rockies and Lake Athabasca in the period just before Europeans arrived.

They were part of the larger language group termed "Athapaskan," which is thought to have originated in Alaska, then to have splintered into several groups. Athapaskans broke into dialects that reached across Western Canada and into the United States. It is a measure of Athapaskan flexibility that the splinter groups include not only the Beaver, Chipewyan and the Slavey of the boreal forest and the Sarsi

148

of central and southern Alberta, but also the Navajo and Apache of the American southwest.

The Algonkian-speaking Cree Indians, who occupied much of northern Alberta during the fur trade, are believed to be late-comers to this part of the boreal forest. They acquired firearms sometime before 1760, and swept the Beaver Indians from the Athabasca Valley.

The prehistoric Athapaskans did not leave many identifiable traces. But their living legacy of adaptability provides some of our best clues about how prehistoric people lived in the boreal forest.

Strategies for Survival

Even today, fierce winter storms can close schools, halt traffic and disrupt modern life in dozens of ways across Alberta. Freezing temperatures as late as June and as early as August are not uncommon. How did the Athapaskans crack such a hostile world so long before central heating, goose-down parkas and snowmobiles?

One way was by mastering snow. It was once thought that severe cold posed the major challenge for early northerners — a challenge they partly met by producing warm clothing of leather and fur, and shelters made of wooden frames and covered with tanned skins. Now, it appears, that learning to deal with the snow was the more critical adaptation.

Just as the stilt-like legs of the moose; the long, wide hind feet of the snowshoe hare; and, the splayed hooves of the caribou equip them for fast movement through snow, Athapaskans manufactured snowshoes of leather and wood to move about in the deep powdery snow of the forest. They also made toboggans, but not skis.

The same snow that hindered movement also helped the hunters track game. Moose, likely the most prized game, would literally drop from exhaustion after being pursued for fifteen kilometres.

The hunter's mind, however, proved far more important than speed. The Athapaskans, like their Algonkian neighbours in the more easterly forest, possess a surpassing knowledge of how to survive in a wide territory of scattered resources and ever-changing conditions.

As Don Dumond of the University of Oregon sees it, this

Snare. The animal is caught in the loop as it passes through.

is the intellectual aspect of Athapaskan life. It was not so much that Athapaskans ate fish and hunted rabbits, but rather, it was what they could do with the knowledge in their heads and a bit of sinew and fur that they carried with them.

As much as they sometimes stored food, subarctic Athapaskans were inclined to "store" knowledge. For example, they fixed in their memories the territories of bears. A bear caught hibernating in winter was an easy target for a tired, hungry hunter. This was perhaps the Athapaskan equivalent of saving for a rainy day.

They fashioned complex varieties of snares to catch small game such as hare, grouse and beaver. They made nets out of willow and the roots of spruce trees. Bone and stone tools included hide-scrapers, needles and fleshers. They used their knowledge of animal behaviour to develop sophisticated means of tracking game.

As mentioned, one of the chief problems facing subarctic hunters is that of fluctuating game populations. The densities of snowshoe hare, for example, can vary by as much as twenty-fold in ten-year cycles. Populations of lynx, fox, hawks and other hare predators fluctuate along with the wildly swinging cycles of the snowshoe hare. The populations of caribou and moose also exhibit marked, though less regular, swings.

"A plot of forest that supports four lynx in times of plenty may bring one of them through the lean years, or none at all," noted Candace Savage in *Wild Mammals of Western Canada.* "Such cyclical oscillation in lynx numbers, synchronized over vast areas of Canada, can be traced back in the fur trade records for two centuries."

Seasonal rounds were, and are critical to survival in this huge snowy world of dispersed resources. The Athapaskans operated with one of the lowest population densities in the world — approximately one person every 150 square kilometres. Only arid parts of Western Australia can approach such low densities. In a constantly-changing environment, the Athapaskans had to figure out which resource to exploit, when and where.

When game failed in winter, ice fishing lakes and rivers became critical. People also moved to lakes or streams where they knew pike, whitefish or grayling were spawning. In the fall, when nighttime temperatures fell below freezing and some game moved into lowlands such as the Peace and Athabasca river valleys, they would follow. Winter likely found them in a sheltered area with plenty of firewood; during spring break-up they may have gravitated to a fish lake near Lake Athabasca and hunted birds, beavers, and muskrats. By summer, they may have trekked to a lake in the Birch Mountains to fish, visit with relatives and perhaps participate in communal hunts for bison.

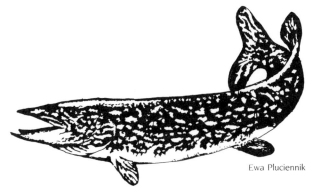

Ewa Pluciennik

Northern Pike

The Athapaskans understood what some of the European polar explorers failed to grasp. They knew that ensuring an adequate diet of fat over the long cold winter is a vital part of winter survival. (In severe conditions, without fat, the digestion of protein runs the body into an energy deficit. In the bush, this is called "rabbit starvation.") In winter, some animals such as moose, caribou and hare, live off fat reserves collected in summer. During a harsh winter in which these animals grew lean, their flesh could not always fill the hunters' fat requirements.

In these conditions beaver and whitefish proved vital. Both keep their fat during the winter, providing needed nourishment to people trying to withstand the draining cold.

Lynx tracks

All these strategies and the reliance on a variety of resources provided extra insurance for the harsh winters — years of sparse snow cover, bitter cold, and low game densities. These were the key problems that northern people in this province had to cope with.

Forest skills, such as the ability to drive beavers from their lodges, could make the difference between survival and death by starvation.

So could foresight. Subarctic peoples practiced their own form of game management long ago. Beaver Indian hunters, for example, would not destroy the entire population of a beaver lodge; some would always be spared so the beaver population might be renewed. This form of custodianship suffered with the arrival of guns and the fur trade in the forest. Today, a strong ethic in game management remains widespread in the north.

The Importance of Social Ties

Although life for northern forest dwellers could be precarious, they possessed a kind of safety net. One family could be related to dozens of other families scattered through the forest — and relatives helped each other in times of need.

These kin ties enabled people to move freely from one area when food supplies dwindled and enter another area where they might be able to get by, or even find a surplus of resources. Just as some African tribes are famed for their ability to name many generations removed from their own, Athapaskans were able to trace and rely upon dozens or hundreds of relatives distributed over enormous geographic areas.

In Athapaskan society, as in other hunter-gatherer societies, food was given freely to others. Successful hunters were recognized for their ability to provide. A kind of status could be achieved based on the individual's ability to serve the rest of society. Nevertheless, good hunters might not have eaten any better than the worst. At the same time, better hunters had more to redistribute, investing the giver with a subtle hold over the receiver.

Like hunter-gatherers all over the world, the Athapaskans divided themselves into local and regional groups. The small local groups consisted of approximately twenty-five to eighty people and larger groups from 400 to 500.

Local groups gathered within a region at certain times of the year, probably summer, seeking reacquaintance with relatives, marriage and information about game. Individuals would learn where other groups planned to spend the rest of the year, and likely held in their memories detailed information about the winter itineraries of several groups. This amounted to a form of prehistoric life insurance — they worked out in advance where to go for help if winter in their own area proved dire.

Muskrat tracks

A Spiritually-Charged World

Life in the prehistoric woods held a deeper dimension than merely setting snares and scraping caribou hides. A spiritual bond with the world of the forest was established. Some would call it magic.

Unfortunately, few clues allow Alberta archaeologists to study in detail the spiritually-charged dimensions of life in the boreal forest. So far, any indications supporting this aspect of prehistoric life are limited to the plains, with its better preserved and more visible archaeological record. There is no reason to suppose, however, that spirituality was of any less importance in the forest.

In Athapaskan society, for instance, boys would set out on vision quests with the object of finding a spiritual "ally" to help guide them in their hunts — a quest similar to that of their adolescent counterparts on Alberta's Plains.

The Beaver also invoked forms of magic. There are Beaver hunters known today who dream of the spirit of the moose they kill the next day. Before killing the animal, the hunters thank it for offering itself to them. There are also written accounts of divination, where Cree or other Algonkians burned moose bones before a hunt and read the location of game from patterns on the bone.

Adrian Tanner, a specialist on the Cree of northern Quebec, has argued that hunting rested on a social relationship between men and animals. During hunting, hunters emphasize their respect to the hunted; after the killing, the corpse is treated like a sacred object.

"All this might sound absurd to Western ears, not accustomed to hearing rodents and other wildlife described as sentient beings," noted Calvin Martin in *Keepers of the Game*, his book about Indian-animal relationships.

If some of these ideas suggest the Don Juan figure popularized by Carlos Castaneda, it is because the Native culture of Western Canada reflects similar ideas. The concept of individuality and power, of respecting the needs of animals and recognizing their powers, formed the foundation of much of their world view.

Although there is much we do not know about the personal spiritual life so important in Athapaskan society, we do know that animals were invested with personalities. Noted anthropologist Franz Boas offered this definition of such a belief, called *animism*:

> All nature, the heavenly bodies, rocks and islands, waterfalls, animals and plants, are beings of supernatural power, whom man can approach with prayer and whose help he can ask, and to whom he may express his thanks.

The Athapaskans believed in the concept of personal powers gained by the process of vision-questing. (See Chapter 4.) According to the Athapaskans' views of personal power, there was no good or bad luck. A spell of bad hunting was instead viewed as a diminution of the hunter's personal power.

Important figures called tricksters also appear in Native mythology. The Cree, for example, believed that what we now call the Whiskey Jack or Canada Jay — one of the boldest birds of the northern forest — possessed supernatural powers. Like taboos and spiritually powerful shaman, tricksters are part of a complex set of myths and beliefs which prehistoric forest people held about a world, which to them, was not divided into the natural and the supernatural, as we might have it, but rather was regarded as wholly supernatural.

More Light on the Puzzle

This, then, describes our best estimation of the kind of world the northern forest dwellers inhabited.

The very economic and social strategies that allowed people to live in the northern forest continue to make life difficult for archaeologists investigating that early life. Subarctic Athapaskans and Algonkians adapted to different situations in so many ways that we may only have achieved a tiny glimmer of understanding of the complicated whole.

Yet, there is no need for discouragement. The field of investigation is new — so new that intensive archaeological research in northern Alberta has only taken place in the last fifteen years, spurred by oil sands development. And new imaginative ways are being sought to illuminate the sparse archaeological record left by northern forest dwellers.

That story begins in a soggy patch of muskeg. . . .

Stalking the Canny Moose

The moose, prized among Athapaskan hunters for its meat and hide, possesses a wily strategy to evade predators in the northern forests.

After feeding, the moose's tactic is to double back and rest downwind of its own trail. This enables it to detect the scent of animals or hunters on its trail and to allow time to disappear into the thicker forest.

The Athapaskans devised an ingenious hunting method called semi-circular tracking to take advantage of this habit.

"Instead of following directly in the animal's track, the Indian makes semi-circular detours or loops downwind away from the trail, returning to it at intervals," writes Richard K. Nelson in *Hunters of the Northern Forest*.

"If he circles back and does not find the trail where it should be, he knows the moose has doubled back."

The hunter stalks back in smaller semi-circles until he finds the point where the moose doubled back. He would then expect to find the animal secreted in cover provided by the bush.

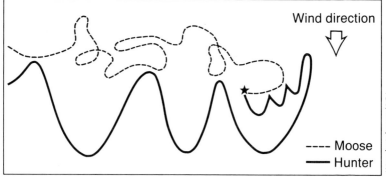

Wind direction

---- Moose
—— Hunter

Wendy Johnson/ASA

Stalking a moose. The hunter periodically locates the animal's trail until he no longer finds it, then backtracks to the animal's location.

Snowshoes: Magic Footwear of the Forest

Prehistoric survival in the snowy northern forests depended in part on tying two pieces of wood together with leather. In a word, *snowshoes.*

"The invention of the snowshoe ranks with the invention of the wheel," maintains Gerry Wolfram in *Walk into Winter.* "There is still no better way to navigate rugged country on foot."

No one is certain where or when the snowshoe originated, although evidence points to Central Asia 6,000 years ago. Prehistoric farmers in Sweden, Norway, northern Spain and Tibet used them. So did North American Natives from the Atlantic to the Rockies — and none more expertly than the Athapaskans and Algonkians.

Shapes varied depending on snow conditions. The deeper and softer the snow, the wider the snowshoe. The more open the country, and harder-packed the snow, the longer and more ski-like the snowshoe.

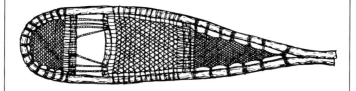

Example of a round toe snowshoe.

Some were rounded, some oval, some shaped like hour-glasses. Some Alaskan snowshoes, for example, are up to three metres long, rather like skis. Many Athapaskans, even today, make two kinds of snowshoes, longer and wider ones for moving over fresh snow while hunting, and sturdier, smaller trail shoes with a pointed toe.

It is thought northern people fashioned snowshoes out of birch, which slides easily over snow. Shoes were laced with deer, moose and caribou leather, and worn with moccasins.

157

Snowshoes not only enabled northern hunters to run down moose in deep snow, but gave them the mobility they needed to set snares for small game in the powdery forest snow. Hand-pulled sleds were also used.

Modern technology has not improved much on tradition. Although today's raciest snowshoes may be molded from the same plastics used for astronaut's helmets, the basic design has changed little.

World of Snow

Snow is snow, right?

Wrong. Prehistoric forest dwellers understood that the word "snow" is an umbrella term for dozens of different kinds of formations and landscapes. Just as rain can mean showers, a drizzle, sleet or monsoons, snow can mean everything from the moist white stuff children make snowballs out of to crusty, cement-like surfaces which easily support the weight of several people.

Variation in snow begins almost from the instant of formation. Snow is defined as precipitation in the form of ice crystals, only usually hexagonal or always so and intricately branched, which form directly from the freezing of water vapour in the air. The fluffy snowfalls so popular on Christmas cards are made up of large, complex snow crystals which form in fairly warm cloud temperatures. The lower temperatures and smaller amounts of moisture over the Arctic result in smaller, harder crystals.

On the ground, snow surfaces are transformed again — depending on temperatures, wind condition and age. Sun crusts are created, for example, when surface crystals repeatedly melt and freeze. Wind crust is caused by the mechanical action of the wind. Astonishingly, the hardness of wind-packed snow can be up to 50,000 times that of fluffy, light snow.

Identifying kinds of snow and learning their properties was critical to life in both the Arctic and the subarctic boreal forest. The Chipewyan of northern Alberta, for example, use as many as thirteen terms to describe various snow conditions. There is one for snow that collects on trees, and other words for fluffy snow, wind-beaten snow, drift, snow deep enough for snowshoes, sun-crusted snow, snow which persists all summer and, bowl-shaped depressions in snow found around the base of trees.

Snowgoggles

Both subarctic and Arctic peoples needed these distinctions to survive. In the forest, hoofed animals such as moose can speed through powdery snow with their stilt-like legs. They do not fare nearly so well over crusty snow which cuts into their fetlocks. "On the wind-hardened snow of the open Arctic tundra the Inuit sled, or 'komatik' rides upon runners and is unsurpassed in lightness, ruggedness and ease of pulling," William O. Pruitt of the University of Manitoba has written:
"For the thick, fluffy snows of the subarctic forest, where the komatik would bog down, the Indians created the runnerless toboggan."
In the far north, Inuit could walk on most snow-packed surfaces without sinking and, cut blocks of snow to build the houses we know as igloos. Not so in the boreal forest, where forest dwellers devised snowshoes and relied on shelters of wood and hide. Forest dwellers were keenly aware of a wealth of life under the snow. Only relatively large animals such as the wolf, lynx and hare are able to withstand winter above the snow surface. Beneath, small animals such as voles and shrews, and insects such as spiders and fleas survive under the insulating cover of snow.

Pruitt notes that snow is such an effective insulator that temperatures on the mossy forest floor seldom drop below minus six degrees Celsius (twenty degrees Fahrenheit), although the air above may be minus fifty-one Celsius (minus sixty Fahrenheit). He calls snow ''one of life's most interesting provinces.'' Life, in this province of snow, demanded its mastery.

Peace Point:
A Stratified Site in the Boreal Forest

One of the difficulties faced by archaeologists working in the boreal forest is finding well-stratified sites — sites where artifacts have remained in the same layers of earth they were originally laid.

The major rivers of the north, as well as some other areas like the Athabasca sand dunes, deposit sediments in some places. The problem, however, is to find localities frequently occupied by humans in which deep deposits are created and protected. We won't know more about the chronological framework of the boreal forest—the sequence of events in prehistory—until we find and excavate such deeply-buried sites.

Archaeologist Ruth Gruhn of the University of Alberta recognized this problem while working at Calling Lake, Alberta. She concluded: ''Boreal Forest archaeologists must fall back upon the admittedly very dubious practice of extrapolation of the age of diagnostic point types from dated sites elsewhere to the finds in the undated context.''

Husband and colleague Alan Bryan showed this at the Karpinsky Site near Wanham. Large, stemmed points, quite like Paleo-Indian points, turned out to be scarcely a thousand years old, once dated.

Although stratified sites may be a relatively rare occurrence in the boreal forest, the archaeological deposits at Peace Point on the lower Peace River show that such sites do exist. At some time prior to Pond's penetration of the Athabasca region in 1778, the Beaver and Cree Indians arranged a truce, thereby ending warfare which had extended throughout the protohistoric period. This event took place at Peace Point. Marc Stevenson, then with Parks Canada, undertook excavations which showed that Peace Point is in fact a magnificent archaeological site.

Beginning just over 2,200 years ago, river sediments began to accumulate at Peace Point. Stevenson found eighteen distinct occupation surfaces embedded within these deposits formed over a series of ancient soils. Abundant stone artifacts, numerous features such as hearths, and an inventory of well-preserved bones including bison, moose, caribou, elk, black and grizzly bear, beaver, muskrat, waterfowl and fish, were also discovered.

Frequent accumulation of sediments at Peace Point also made for a record of great fidelity. One occupation surface at the site appeared to preserve, in a pattern of waste stone flakes, the outline of the kneeling craftsman!

Unfortunately, Stevenson's work yielded only one projectile point from a very recent period.

Nevertheless, it is through more excavation at Peace Point and similar sites that archaeologists will eventually flesh out the prehistory of the boreal forest.

cm

Four microblade cores and a reconstructed microcore from the Bezya site.

6

Muskeg to Microblades: The Northern People

One summer day in 1980, the whirr of a helicopter broke the peace of a remote patch of northern Alberta forest. Within a few minutes, the helicopter landed on the spongy muskeg and an archaeological field crew of four disembarked in the midst of desolation. Their position was ten kilometres from the Athabasca River, sixty kilometres north of Fort McMurray and 440 kilometres northeast of Edmonton.

Shovels in hand, the crew headed for nearby knolls of aspen and pine to begin their search. Moving proved difficult. With each step their boots dipped into muskeg. Peat bogs, perhaps 8,000 to 10,000-years-old, lay a few metres beneath the mossy surface. Blackflies and mosquitoes followed in pesky swarms.

The team's search was far from haphazard — aerial analysis had earlier identified several knolls likely to provide artifacts. Remote as the location was, it would soon provide evidence which could help answer how people patterned their life in these forests thousands of years ago. . .

The Beaver River Sandstone Mystery

By 1980, archaeologists were aware of a peculiar trend in a pocket of northeastern Alberta. Nearly 300 archaeological sites had been discovered on oil sands leases in the Athabasca Valley north of Fort McMurray. Surface collections and scientific excavations had discovered tens of thousands of artifacts.

Yet, almost all the artifacts were either impossible to date or, if they could be dated, were mixed with artifacts of radically different ages. Almost all were literally rubbish — the flakes and debris of stone tool manufacture, rather than finished tools.

What intrigued scientists was that most of these traces of prehistoric life were composed of a distinctive kind of hard siliceous stone called *Beaver River Sandstone* (BRS).

One source, the Beaver River Quarry near Fort MacKay, had been identified. Could one source explain the thousands of other sandstone flakes showing up all over the muskeg-ridden valley? Some Beaver River Sandstone had appeared seventy kilometres northwest in the Birch Mountains and some as far south as the present site of Devon, near Edmonton. How did it get there?

It boiled down to this: if archaeologists knew for certain where Beaver River Sandstone came from, they might also learn more about the seasonal movements of prehistoric forest dwellers.

Over the next few pages, we shall follow the deductive reasoning which led modern-day archaeologists to some illuminating answers. An unlikely event — the work of a highway crew — pointed the way.

Hints From Today, Yesterday and Long Ago

Clues from three dramatically different time periods, reaching from the Mesozoic age to modern-day development, came together to provide a possible solution to the puzzle.

First, Alberta was experiencing an oil boom. Oil prices hit more than thirty-five dollars a barrel; skylines in booming Calgary and Edmonton were jammed with the silhouettes of construction cranes.

Both the Syncrude plant and the proposed Alsands plant near Fort McMurray held hope for sustaining the province's economic growth. Everything was happening quickly.

With the prospect of four or five oil sands plants in the hitherto-undeveloped Athabasca Valley, work began on numerous studies to assess potential impact on environmental and historical resources in the area. By the spring of 1980, Alsands had spent nine-million dollars clearing forest land for development. Archaeologists hurried out to chart what

Mark Fenton sampling Beaver River Sandstone.

archaeological resources, if any, should be protected from the massive development.

Long before modern technology made oil sands extraction economically feasible, however, both prehistoric and historic man had discovered practical uses for it. The first accounts from York Factory, between 1714-15, mention the oil sands. Later records allude to Natives' use of a sticky, tarry substance for patching canoes.

The discovery of the Beaver River Quarry in 1972 showed another application. The remains of a huge open-air workshop where stone tools were made had been discovered on a neighbouring Syncrude lease along the Beaver River, and excavated in 1973. Scientists who examined the large toolmaking site even found evidence, in the form of an Agate Basin projectile point, of use of the area 8,000 to 10,000 years ago. They believed the workshops had seen most activity in the last two thousand years, indicated by a projectile point rather like the Besant style.

What made Beaver River Quarry most interesting was the fact it yielded a distinctive kind of hard sandstone, suitable

Exposed seam of Beaver River Sandstone.

for stone tool manufacture, which became known as Beaver River Sandstone. Soon Beaver River Sandstone started showing up all over the region.

The third time zone in the puzzle lay far, far back in time, as long as 400 million years ago.

This important connection might never have been known but for a fortunate accident in 1980. A highway crew, looking for more gravel for a road, spotted rubble on the lease where the Beaver River Quarry had been excavated.

They proceeded to dynamite a hole ten metres deep at the north edge of the site, for a borrow pit. The debris was carted off to be crushed into gravel. This activity exposed the mother lode of Beaver River Sandstone below the forest floor.

Narrowing in on the Answer

Oil industry geologists had shown little interest in exploring the source deposits of Beaver River Sandstone. The deposits lie just above the bedrock basement of the area, and the finer oil sands deposits beneath the Beaver River Sandstone have little economic value.

However, this did not deter the archaeologists. Once the

Beaver River Quarry construction incident revealed what the source of sandstone looked like, and where it could be found, interest heightened in tapping the region's geological past to shed light on its human past.

Field crews under the direction of Jack Ives of the ASA and geologist Mark Fenton, of the Terrain Sciences Department of the Alberta Research Council, conducted an extensive search for other sources. They used trucks to search roads and trails, and canoes and boats to scan river banks.

The approach worked. Before long, Ives and Fenton not only knew where Beaver River Sandstone came from, but more importantly, where it *did not* come from.

Tracking Beaver River Sandstone starts with understanding events which occurred about 400 million to 375 million years ago. At that time a huge sea covered the interior of North America from Alaska down to Arizona and California. Clams, corals and other shell-like sea creatures were deposited on the sea bottom over many thousands of years. The accumulating weight of these sediments caused the deposits to be compressed into limestone. With time, the sea retreated. The exposed limestone was then eroded by a unique process. When carbon dioxide in air is mixed with water, a weak solution of carbonic acid forms. Over millions of years, this solution ate away calcareous deposits, just as chalk reacts with vinegar.

The result? This Devonian limestone "basement" eroded into an irregular surface marked with caves, holes and pockets, not unlike Swiss cheese, called *karst* topography.

This limestone surface is exposed at some places in the Fort MacKay area, but at most locations it is buried by the later *McMurray Formation*. Geologists call the old karst surface an "unconformity" because the erosion which occurred at that time created a gap in the sediments. We have no record for that period because geologists have no deposits to study. Thus, it is difficult to say when sediments were redeposited to become the McMurray Formation, but this likely began 125 million years ago or more. The inland sea appeared again, and alternately covered the entire area or parts nearby. When nearby, this region served as the delta for a river which flowed into the sea. Ultimately, the sands and silts of this McMurray Formation became impregnated with oil, forming the oil sands we know today.

Ives and Fenton realized that the sandstone tools employed hundreds and thousands of years ago by prehistoric people were shaped from rock formed many millions of years ago.

Beaver River Sandstone, it turned out, is really a "barren oil sand." Some sediments in the lower part of the McMurray Formation were infused not with oil but with silica, a hard substance which is the major mineral constituent in most of the stones prehistoric craftsmen used to make tools. The Beaver River Sandstone unit is exposed in some areas of the Athabasca Valley, but not in others, owing to the irregular bedrock beneath it.

The hunt began. Crews, which now had an idea of where and what to look for, patrolled up and down the Athabasca Valley looking for Beaver River Sandstone exposures along the Athabasca River and its tributaries. They also scoured roads and gravel pits in the region. In the end, a handful of source areas were found.

The geological information and the fieldwork indicated that Beaver River Sandstone is confined in its natural occurrences to the Athabasca River Valley, where the Athabasca and its tributaries have cut deeply. Centred in the Fort MacKay region, it disappears to the north, and is deeply buried both east and west of the Athabasca River. (Its southward boundary is hazier. There could be Beaver River Sandstone sources along the Clearwater River where similarly aged deposits also occur.)

The most intriguing conclusion? Fenton and Ives are sure Beaver River Sandstone could not have occurred naturally in the Birch Mountains area, one or more days' journey on foot from Fort MacKay. There, it is under 500 metres of sediment.

The Meaning of the Birch Mountains Connection

The pieces of the puzzle started to come together. Partly, it was a matter of analyzing statistics. Ives began to compare the kinds and numbers of Beaver River Sandstone artifacts found throughout the region.

Abundant quantities appeared in the Athabasca River Valley around Fort MacKay. Evidence of all parts of the tool-making process, from scarcely modified cores of raw material to projectile points, had been uncovered. At many sites, all or almost all of the artifacts were made of Beaver River Sandstone.

The number of sandstone artifacts, however, tapered off beyond a radius of about thirty kilometres from the Fort MacKay region of the Athabasca River. About seventy kilometres farther northwest in the Birch Mountains, Beaver River Sandstone tools are present, but only in small amounts and as smaller artifacts. Moreover, the kind of artifacts unearthed suggest that only worn-out or broken tools, or smaller flakes from sharpening tools, were left behind.

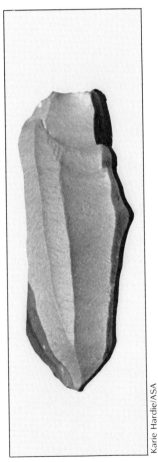 

Karie Hardie/ASA

Karie Hardie/ASA

(Left) Face on view of a microblade core from the Bezya site. Microblades were removed from the flutes which are visible. (Right) Microblades from the Bezya Site.

One way archaeologists gauge the intensity of stone tool manufacture is to compare the amount of discarded by-products (flakes and fragments) from tool manufacture to the number of finished tools. Just as sawdust can be a rough indicator of a carpenter's activity, so numerous flakes or debris indicate copious tool-making. In the Birch Mountains, the ratio for Beaver River Sandstone is extremely low: about five or six flakes or other by-products for every completed tool. In the Athabasca River Valley it is far higher, with between fifty to 100 or more by-product items for every finished product.

So rare are finished tools in the Athabasca Valley that less than twenty projectile points have been found in perhaps a quarter of a million artifacts. In contrast, a relatively small amount of archaeological work carried out in the Birch Mountains has yielded between 150 to 200 points of various raw materials including Beaver River Sandstone.

All this together can help to explain how prehistoric people planned their seasonal movements in the northeastern forest.

Seasonal Rounds and Settlement Strategies

From the Beaver River Sandstone evidence and from ecological information, it seems likely prehistoric people in the Athabasca Valley incorporated the Birch Mountains into their seasonal rounds for thousands of years. The belief is they chose spring or early summer for their trek into the uplands because game was most abundant then and fish ran plentifully in spawns. In winter, game became scarce. Woodland bison and moose, for example, move out of the Birch Mountains in winter and return in spring. Prehistoric people likely fished the lakes in the Birch Mountains as an emergency resource if starvation threatened during hard winter months.

How did scientists arrive at such a conclusion on the basis of tool-making debris? First, the Beaver River Sandstone items are utilitarian and do not occur at too great a distance from their geological sources.

Second, they reasoned that when hunters who were camped in the Athabasca Valley ran out of raw material for their tools, their supplies could easily be replenished on the next hunting or trapping trip near a source.

Beyond a certain point, the trip back would simply not be worthwhile. Instead, Ives reasons, hunters would begin using up the Beaver River Sandstone tools they had, sharpening the stone, breaking others and so on. Other, closer raw materials would be used to make new stone tools. The small amount of Beaver River Sandstone in the Birch Mountains, therefore, appears simply to reflect distance from quarry sites, and the tendency for tools to reach the end of their use in the Birch Mountains.

This evidence also suggests the predominance of a way of life in which small family groups foraged widely, as opposed to the communal hunting of the plains. Communal hunters often set the stage for bison kills by "gearing up." Larger numbers of people travelled to quarries to manufacture the many tools required to kill and process the animals in a successful hunt. Such traces have not yet been found in the boreal forest.

The pattern suggests another clue. Although people moved widely between the Athabasca Valley and the Birch Mountains, the small amount of Beaver River Sandstone they carried suggests they took an indirect route. They appear to have taken sufficient time journeying from the valley to the upland Birch Mountains, to use up almost completely the stash of Beaver River Sandstone tools they had.

The work of the scientific crew we left on a remote knoll in the forest in 1980, helps to explain in greater detail how Beaver River Sandstone flowed from geological sources, through the tool kits of prehistoric peoples and into the archaeological record.

The Lesson of Alsands

The *knolls* on the Alsands lease were undoubtedly part of seasonal rounds which took prehistoric peoples from the lowlands of the Athabasca Valley in winter to fish the lakes of the Birch Mountains in summer.

In the northern forest, knolls stand out as comforting islands in a sea of muskeg. For people in need of a camp, they offer treed shelter and firewood. Moreover, with snowshoes and toboggans, they are easily reached in winter. Better-drained, they are home to a variety of vegetation including aspen, jackpine, willows, berries, rosebushes and some grasses.

In an important way, these "islands" are in constant change. Tree cover on knolls and ridges can be destroyed by fire, insects or high winds. Sun-loving tree species, such as aspen, flourish after such destruction. Pine and aspen both have an advantage following a fire. Aspen suckers leap up from roots, while fire releases seeds from resin-sealed pine cones. More shade-tolerant spruces eventually supplant these species. This process, called *succession*, makes for a patchy environment with plant communities in many stages of development.

Plant cover on these knolls, especially in early stages of succession, provides much more food and shelter for animals than muskeg can. An animal such as a moose may spend as much as ninety per cent of its time on these knolls and ridges in fall and winter, browsing, resting and rutting.

When archaeologists surveyed the great cleared area (thirteen square kilometres) at Alsands, this pattern held. Trowels and rakes uncovered isolated finds with only a single tool or a flake. They also uncovered quite large sites with hundreds, even thousands of artifacts. The Bezya site, discovered earlier by the 1980 crew, was unique because it ultimately yielded every aspect of a blade technology, including five microcores, microblades and *burins*, which are chisel-like tools.

Archaeologists discovered an average of one site for every terrain feature. A long ridge, for example, might house three or four sites, and three or four other knolls might yield nothing.

Some sites, like Bezya, proved larger and more complex than others. The probable explanation is that prehistoric people used the larger ones as residential camps in winter, since knoll sites would have provided both shelter and firewood. The lengthy distance to a source of water would not have mattered then, since snow would simply have been melted.

The small sites, with just a few artifacts, quite likely record activities such as moose-hunting and the trapping of fur-bearing animals.

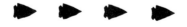

The Task Ahead

The preceding case study should leave no doubt about the difficulties the boreal forest poses for archaeologists.

Stone artifacts are plentiful, but acidic soils make preservation poor. Often artifacts, such as bone from butchered animals, are absent from the archaeological record. Moreover, archaeologists often cannot determine the age of these artifacts.

"I think it is precisely these difficulties which make archaeological work in the region challenging," says Ives. "Inasmuch as the archaeological record uncovered is reduced to its bare essentials, research in northern Alberta must make maximal use of that information which is present.

"When we do this, meaningful insights into the past come about. The scant assemblages from the Alsands knolls, often little more than a few flakes or part of a biface, record the briefest instants in time. They are the material record of events like the successful hunter, dressing out his moose."

In this study, clues from geology, modern-day industry and the fur-trading days combined to shed light on prehistoric settlement patterns in the Athabasca River Valley.

More ways must be found to extract the forest's tale. Only by such efforts can a full understanding of the rich texture of prehistoric life in northern Alberta be achieved — a way of life that was about to change as Pond stood on the summit of Methy Portage.

Microblades and the Art of Stone Tool-Making

A well-known archaeologist, facing open-heart surgery, handed a stone blade to his surgeon to use in place of a scalpel.

The archaeologist knew that such a blade, when made from a black volcanic glass called obsidian, cuts more cleanly than even the finest metal edge. Smaller blades have even been used in eye surgery. Only recent laser technology has produced cleaner incisions.

Prehistoric people manufactured such miniature blades, called *microblades*, which are only three to five millimetres wide and about twenty millimetres long. Their manufacture, from raw materials including obsidian and chert represents one of the greatest refinements in stone tool-making.

In Alberta, microblade technology is best represented at a small site called Bezya ("Little Knife" in Chipewyan). *Microcores*, from which the microblades were made, microblades themselves, burins and scrapers were among the finds.

Making microblades required highly-skilled craftsmen with a well-conceived plan of attack. Fortunately, many of the blades and flakes from Bezya could be pieced back together with their cores, so the stages of microblade production could be reconstructed with great accuracy.

These microblade craftsmen of long ago selected waterworn chert pebbles, from local gravel deposits, for cores. Detailed analysis by archaeologists showed that they shaped the cores by trimming two perpendicular and adjacent edges. Ridges were carefully chipped on these edges. Then a long flake from the top ridge was removed, creating a smooth platform from which blades could be pressed with a pointed instrument. Next, another long flake was detached along the perpendicular ridge. This produced a long flake scar with nearly parallel edges. The long scar was used to guide removal of a series of blades. Whenever the platform deteriorated, a new, long flake would be removed across the top of the pebble, and the process of removing microblades could begin again. Eventually, the microcore would become so reduced it was discarded.

Many of the microblades at Bezya appear entirely unused. In other parts of the world (such as the Canadian Arctic and Europe), microblades were slotted along the edge of bone and antler tools to create a continuous cutting edge. In fact, the microblade method of manufacture provided a far greater amount of cutting edge. It is estimated that one kilogram of stone would yield more than 100 metres of cutting edge. This is many times more than the yield of other flaking technologies.

Few microcore specimens are known. It is possible that the Bezya microcores were simply trade items, in which case they need not indicate actual population movements or even extensive cultural interaction.

Evidence of microblade technology in northeastern Alberta may nevertheless represent the most extreme eastward extension of a particular microblade-manufacturing tradition found throughout northwestern North America, according to Raymond Le Blanc and Jack Ives.

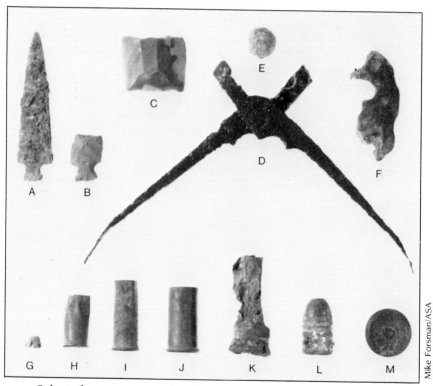

Selected armaments and related artifacts from Victoria Post, Hudson's Bay Company. A) Metal point, B) Stone point, C) Gun flint, D) Shot mould, E) Musket ball, F) Side plate, G-K) Shell casings, L) Shell, M) Bottom of cartridge.

7

Historical Archaeology in Alberta

It was early morn, but up went the flag, and the little metropolis was all excitement in consequence of our arrival. The Chief Factor in those days was supreme in his own district... No wonder the ... fort was en fête when such ecclesiastical and commercial dignity came suddenly upon it.
- Missionary John McDougall on arrival at Rocky Mountain House with Chief Factor William Christie, 1865

The story of the first 100 years of European occupation in Alberta is the story of the fur trade. In 1778, Peter Pond built the first fur trade post in present-day Alberta. Called Pond's Fort, it was situated on the Athabasca River, about sixty kilometres south of Lake Athabasca.

The rich furs of the Athabasca and Saskatchewan districts combined with intense rivalry between the Hudson's Bay Company and the North West Company saw an explosion of other posts strung out along the Athasbasca, Peace and North Saskatchewan Rivers.

The fur traders brought with them the written word. But these words were designed specific to their own ends — not necessarily for historical accuracy. The historical record of the period must therefore be fleshed out by archaeological research. It is a discipline called *historical archaeology*.

Archaeology of the Fur-Trading Posts

This kind of fascinating research has the challenge of uncovering and interpreting details about the more than sixty trade posts erected in Alberta over the 200 years since the time of Peter Pond. Most were built before 1821, when the two feuding companies amalgamated.

Research is most concentrated in the northern half of the province where the rich fur resources were located. Karlis Karklins, for example, has conducted extensive archaeological investigations of Nottingham House, the Hudson's Bay Company fort in the Athabasca region occupied between 1802 and 1806.

The chief posts were Fort Chipewyan in the Athabasca district and Fort Edmonton in the Saskatchewan district. Both were large, elaborate facilities with considerable historical documentation about them. But many outposts were roughly hacked out of the forest and used for only one season. Less than half of the sixty posts have been found and only sixteen excavated.

One of the basic and vital functions of historic archaeologists (although certainly not the only one), is to fill in the gaps in written records. The majority of documents belonging to the North West Company, for example, were destroyed upon amalgamation with the Hudson's Bay Company.

Another difficulty is that written records offer few insights into day to day life on the frontier. One writer, Duncan McGillivray, a Scottish-born clerk with the North West Company, kept a journal during his two years at Fort George, and wrote frequently of fur resources and other business aspects of fort life. Only rarely did he give any information about the fort itself.

Commenting on the importance of archaeological investigation into the early fur trade sites of Alberta, Robert Kidd, as curator of archaeology for the Provincial Museum and Archives, once wrote: "Evidence for the ground plan or for specific structural features in the available journal material pertaining to Fort George is extremely scarce. . . structural data must presently be derived from archaeological evidence."

Fort George: A Story in a Chink of Mud

The task facing archaeologists is to sift through wood remains, cellar depressions, fireplaces, mud chinks, glass fragments and other clues, in order to reconstruct what Fort George looked like. The fort, built by the North West Company in 1792, is located on the north bank of the North Saskatchewan River, forty-eight kilometres west of the present-day Alberta-Saskatchewan border and twelve kilometres southeast of Elk Point.

Few of us would have any use for mud recovered from the site of a burned-down fur-trading fort. To an archaeologist, however, the eighty-five boxes full of fired mud chinking from Fort George are far from mute.

Fort Dunvegan

Once plastered to the outside of the fort's main house, the mud naturally survived a fire which razed the fort. Negative impressions in the mud illustrate some of the construction techniques employed in building the main house where the chief factor, chief traders and clerks lived. Other evidence of fort construction comes from remains in the ground.

Mud taken from elsewhere in the fort indicates far less time and craft was expended in building barracks for lowly labourers. This is information one probably would not obtain

179

from reading diaries, letters and other historical accounts. One has to turn to archaeology.

The trading posts — each a world to itself — were centres for the bulk of Europeans in Alberta until as late as the 1870s. Fort residents experienced one of North America's last frontiers.

Within the walls dwelled bush-wise French-Canadian voyageurs, taciturn Orkney boatmen, British clerks wielding feather pens, Scottish-born chief factors in top hats, their wives and sometimes their children. Written records, however, were usually kept by only the more privileged participants of the fur trade, and reveal little about life among lower ranks.

Again, archaeology can help to fill in the blanks. Archaeological research indicates that not all forts — or fort occupants — were equal.

Heinz Pyszczyk, an historical archaeologist with the ASA says:

> Some forts, and their respective occupants, were more important, more powerful and much higher in overall prestige in the fur trade . . . These were the forts which controlled the fur trade of large areas and also controlled the flow of resources and information in those respective areas and among their occupants.

Key administrative forts such as the North West Company's Fort Chipewyan on Lake Athabasca and the Hudson's Bay Company's Fort Edmonton enjoyed more privileges than small provisioning forts whose main function was to provide northern forts with pemmican.

But status differentiation occurred at smaller forts as well. Part of Pyszczyk's research involved studying the bones of animals found outside Fort George to determine whether upper ranks ate better than lower ranks.

He further notes that at Fort Dunvegan in the Peace River district, in the later part of the fur trade: ". . . the investment of additional labour and resources into a more elaborate factor's house and warehouses was considered to be more important than improving the living conditions for the men."

The archaeological records of even minor outposts such as Victoria Post reveal status distinctions that would otherwise have been lost in time. The insights gained from archaeology thus hold hope of providing a sharper reflection of the day to day life in Alberta's first European settlers, from the kinds of dwellings they lived in to the types of pipes they smoked.

The Missionaries Arrive

The mid-nineteenth century heralded the beginnings of great changes in Alberta. By the 1850s, free traders began to compete seriously with the Hudson's Bay Company's monopoly on the fur trade. The company fought back by opening new posts, such as Fort Victoria.

The forces which would steer Alberta from a bison and fur-based economy, however, were already at hand. Smallpox, scarlet fever, the re-introduction of liquor and declining bison herds were beginning to pull Native peoples from their traditional, nomadic way of life. The arrival of settlers was not long off.

St. Charles Catholic Mission at Dunvegan. To the left is the Rectory and the chapel is on the right.

Added to those forces, missionaries arrived in the Peace River and Athabasca regions in the 1850s and 60s, determined to convince the Indians and Metis to become farmers instead of hunters. These missionaries kept written records, but, along with those of the fur traders, they are incomplete.

Historical archaeologists hope their discipline can someday illuminate the ways of life of Indian and Metis settlements during that era. For example, at Buffalo Lake, a large

Metis community near present-day Stettler, we have only missionaries' accounts to rely on for information about Metis life. Even simple information which the ASA is now collecting, such as the extent and boundaries of the Buffalo Lake colony, will add additional insights about the Metis.

Historical archaeologists are also interested in learning more about the contrast in lifestyles between missionaries and fur traders. Victoria Post and Fort Dunvegan may yield insights. At Dunvegan, for example, both fur traders and Oblate missionaries lived at the site during part of its long occupation from 1805 to 1918.

So far, investigations at Dunvegan are patchy at best. But further work may verify historic evidence about the relationship between missionaries and fur traders — or question this relationship.

Pyszczyk notes the Oblates were known as simple, frugal people, who depended heavily on supplies from the Hudson's Bay Company. Some distinctions in the types of supplies and material culture would be expected if archaeologists were to sample each.

"If not, one thing that the archaeological record might say is that perhaps the external impression of simplicity of life for the Oblates could be confirmed, or perhaps altered, by the evidence of natural remains.

Mike Forsman/ASA

Chamber pot and bedpan associated with the Clerk's House, Victoria Post, Hudson's Bay Company. Both implements were made by Minton, circa 1822-1836.

The Southern Whiskey Posts

Another colourful, if tawdry, chapter in the province's history opened in 1869, with the construction of the first whiskey fort — Fort Whoop-Up — in southern Alberta. By the 1860s, buffalo robes were in great demand in the industrial East, where their leather was used for drive belts in American factories.

The buffalo robe trade, begun by prominent merchants from Fort Benton, Montana, proved so spectacularly successful that 1869 season that it led to other whiskey traders flooding into southern Alberta.

Officially named Fort Hamilton, the fort became known as Fort Whoop-up because of the riotious drinking associated with it. This fort was immediately burnt to the ground by Natives when the traders vacated it in the spring, but on their return, the traders built another fort nearby. This larger and more established fort became the hub of the whiskey trade in southern Alberta.

Unfortunately for archaeologists, the first Fort Whoop-up site eroded into the Oldman River early this century. About one per cent of the second Fort Whoop-up has been excavated, chiefly to verify its location and size, and to obtain a small sample of the artifacts. Among the artifacts, archaeologists found Perry Davis Vegetable Pain Killer and other alcoholic concoctions which would be mixed with water, whiskey and pepper to produce the liquor that was then traded to the Natives for buffalo robes.

The results of excavations on Fort Whoop-Up point to the need to use some caution when dealing with historical records.

A scale plan of the post, prepared for the North West Mounted Police and bearing the commissioner's stamp, has been preserved. Yet, when the site of the fort was excavated by archaeologists, they found the angle of the drawings was out by ninety degrees. Sifting and probing in the debris of old Alberta forts, therefore, offers a way to test the truth of historic documents.

Although about thirty other whiskey forts were built in southern Alberta, only a handful have been excavated. Less than one per cent of Fort Whoop-Up, for example, has been studied by archaeologists, partly owing to the fact that the site is on private property and would therefore offer few opportunities for development as an interpretive site.

Archaeologists hope, however, that studying these fort sites may someday result in more insight into the extent of American influence on trading goods that long ago. They would expect, for example, to find more goods from American manufacturers, such as handgun and shotgun shells, than they would find in northern Alberta, where the fur-trading companies goods tend to be dominated by English manufacturers.

Police Forts of the South

The days of whiskey forts and lawlessness did not last long. In 1874, after an arduous journey, the North West Mounted Police arrived at Fort Whoop-up to drive away the whiskey traders. That proved short work: they found the fort emptied, the traders having fled.

Construction started immediately on the first police fort in Alberta, on an island on the Oldman River at the present site of Fort Macleod. The police fort itself was moved in 1884; the fort which stands today is only a model.

The remains of two other police forts — one in Fort Saskatchewan and the other at Fort Calgary — have also been studied. Of the three, though, the Fort Macleod site is considered the most important historically and archaeologically.

"Yet ironically, little archaeology has been carried out," says Michael Forsman, with the ASA. He notes that often, archaeological excavation occurs at sites where there is an immediate threat of destruction by impending development. Other sites, safe from such threats, sometimes fail to receive the same amount of attention. This is a common problem faced by archaeologists in many countries.

A second police fort was built in Fort Saskatchewan, on the site of the modern Fort Saskatchewan Correctional Institution, and a limited amount of excavation has been carried out to determine the location of the fort. Fort Calgary, constructed in 1875, in what is today the centre of the city, was for many years built over by railyards. The city of Calgary has since redeveloped the site and established an interpretation centre. Among the smaller police posts, Writing-On-Stone N.W.M.P. post has been the most extensively excavated by Forsman, and Gary Adams, now a Parks Canada archaeologist.

Cattle Ranchers, Settlers and Coal Miners

The presence of the North West Mounted Police, and the establishment of Fort Macleod, Alberta's first town, provided the impetus for cattle ranching in southern Alberta. By the 1880s, large cattle companies sprouted in the western foothills. Many of the early ranchers were in fact former policemen.

Archaeological work at the Cochrane Ranche near Calgary allows visitors to enjoy a first-hand look at the remains of the first large-scale cattle operation in Alberta. In future, it is hoped that historical archaeology can flesh out more of Alberta's colourful ranching past. The Pioneer Ranch, the first ranch in a province famous for its ranches, awaits excavation; so does the Oxley Ranch, a large nineteenth century holding in the Porcupine Hills.

By 1883, the Canadian Pacific Railway was completed as far as Calgary. The Calgary-Edmonton line operating by 1891. Indian reserves had already been established and waves of immigrants arrived to farm lands where nomadic bands had wandered for thousands of years.

One of the challenges of Alberta historical archaeology, which extends well into the twentieth century, is to illuminate *cultural dynamics* — how groups interacted or assimilated. Here, the large influx of Ukrainians to Alberta, (mostly to the Smoky Lake-Vegreville area) may yield insights into such interaction which would be unattainable in any other way.

Alberta archaeologists, for example, are interested in examining how the artifacts and architecture of Ukrainians correspond with their identity or their assimilation into Alberta society. A current ASA project involves collecting artifacts from various Ukrainian farm sites in the Smoky Lake area, and then comparing them to non-Ukrainian artifacts.

Archaeologists are also studying historic coal mining towns in the Crowsnest Pass area of southwestern Alberta. Forsman notes that artifacts from various townsites such as Lille and Frank were found to be fairly similar, but contrasted noticeably with those of the nearby agricultural community of Silcott, Washington. Higher proportions of porcelain wares and imported glasswares and ceramics were present in the

Crowsnest Pass sites, while more beer and wine bottles were discovered at Silcott. The number of olive oil containers recovered from an Italian immigrant section of Lille, showed eating habits not otherwise evident from the historic record, nor as readily observable in the Pass today.

Historical Archaeology and the Public

Historical archaeology plays an important role in fostering public education about the province's heritage, including its industrial past. This is evident at two interpretive centres in the Crowsnest Pass operated by the Historic Site Service. Leitch Collieries, once a sophisticated coal mining and coking operation, for example, is now open to the public during summer months. Another interpretive centre at Frank Slide tells of life in the town devastated by a rock slide early this century. The remains of Bankhead, a coal mining ghost town which thrived between 1904 and 1922, has been developed as a public interpretive site by Parks Canada.

Portion of cellar, Leitch Collieres.

The twentieth century investigations of historical archaeologists in Alberta delve only as close to our time as the 1930s, and include excavations of industrial sites and early agricultural homesteads. Perhaps 100 years from now, the archaeologists of the future will begin digging up sites from the 1950s and 1960s in the continuing search for greater knowledge of Western Canadian culture.

Tales in Trash

Caution about the written word may well be in order if we consider the results of a remarkable study in Tucson, Arizona.

In what came to be called the University of Arizona's Garbage Project, archaeologists collected and analyzed the refuse from over 600 households. Researchers then polled each household about its buying habits. They found a huge gap between what people said they consumed and the story their garbage told.

Only fifteen per cent of the households in one area admitted their occupants drank beer; no household admitted to consumption of more than eight cans a week. More than eighty per cent of the households in the same area, however, threw away beer containers in their garbage. Fifty-four per cent discarded more than eight cans weekly.

The fact people pretended to drink less than they do is not surprising. But the degree of falsehood is startling. This points to the need for some skepticism when examining historical records, and for the sleuthing talents of the historical archaeologist.

Upstairs, Downstairs at Victoria Post

What role did rank play in the day to day life of fur-trading posts?

The Clerks's House at Victoria Post, a minor Hudson's Bay outpost ninety kilometres northeast of present-day Edmonton, provides some clues not contained in historic records.

Victoria Post was built by the Hudson's Bay Company in 1864, one year after Methodist missionary George McDougall established a mission there. Completed in 1865, the Clerk's House is the oldest building in Alberta standing on its original location.

We know almost nothing of the fort occupants and their lifestyles from the historic record. The archaeological record, however, shows that the administrator and his family lived in some style in the middle of the wilderness, with cognac, brass hairbrushes, and clothes trimmed with decorative brass buttons.

Just across the yard, in the men's house, conditions were much different. Labourers had to cook, eat and sleep in small rooms. They also dined from plainer tableware than the residents of the Clerk's House.

The Clerk's House, Victoria Post, Hudson's Bay Company.

Perhaps nowhere are differences in rank as evident as in clothing. Simple utilitarian bone buttons served as the common clothing fastener for residents of the men's house, whereas those in the Clerk's House had their choice of shell buttons, fancy brass buttons and coloured glass buttons. The men even wore brass suspender fasteners while their labourer counterparts used plain buckle fasteners.

The Clerk's House shows evidence of family life. Combs, fragments of jewelry chains and blue-stoned earrings were found. We also gain some insight into spare-time activities. Children played with marbles, dolls and wheeled toys. Someone played a harmonica. The men smoked different kinds of pipes: glazed porcelain pipes were found at the Clerk's House and plain clay ones near the men's house.

The fur trade frontier, for all its romantic aura, was hardly egalitarian. Archaeological findings at Victoria Post indicate sharp distinctions between upper and lower ranks predominated even among a small group of people at a minor outpost.

Says Michael Forsman, an historical archaeologist with the ASA:

> The challenges posed by attempting to explain human behaviour on a late fur trade site like Victoria Post are certainly demanding, but the successes are equally rewarding. Most important for the visitor to the site will be an improved awareness of the ways of life on the Northwest frontier.

Human effigy at British Block Cairn site near Suffield.

ASA

8

The Legacy of the First Albertans

I am happy I still have a (sweat) lodge to go to and people that are still in tune. But the trip from the lodge to the city is one that seems to take thousands of years.
— Architect Douglas Cardinal, from *Of the Spirit*

Even today, the ancient ceremony of the sweat lodge lives on in Alberta. For people like Douglas Cardinal, the great-grandson of a Stoney Indian woman and the first white man to live in the Crowsnest Pass area, the ritual is more than an interesting relic of the past. It is a way of tapping knowledge "beyond the scope of reality" — the same intuitive, spiritual knowledge which helped Natives survive on the plains and in the forests of Alberta for thousands of years.

Other traces of a vanished way of life are also kept alive by Alberta's Natives. Some still climb to remote locations to seek visions, others practice the ancient arts of tipi-making, bone tool-making and sewing leather clothing.

Yet today's treasured traditions can recreate only part of Alberta's mythic, unrecorded past. The archaeological quest for more understanding of that earlier world must continue if we are to gain a fuller appreciation of this province's heritage.

Archaeologist Jack Brink inspects a petroglyph at Head-Smashed-In.

An equally compelling reason for learning about prehistoric Alberta, however, is to provide a link between the twentieth century perspective of the world, and the mysterious, inexplicable view of the universe held by earlier occupants of this province. The Natives who walked the plains and forests so many thousands of years ago appear to have believed in a world in which the universe — the stars, the sun, the moon — were spiritually-charged. Indeed, all living things were thought to contain life forces.

In contrast to the scientific, technological basis of modern-day existence, such a perspective offers a "crack" or glimpse into another view of the universe, to borrow from the terms of author Carlos Castaneda's mystical Don Juan figure. Archaeology, in other words, points back to a world of greater diversity, a world forever changed by the mass culture and mass communications of the global village.

In New Guinea there lives a tribe which has names for only two colours in the world (although they almost certainly do not perceive colours much differently from the rest of us). For people of industrialized nations, who tend to identify the same colours, drink the same brand of soft drink and follow the same American soap operas, the richness of past cultures provides much to savour. Indeed, non-conformity to Western industrial ways is becoming so rare some social scientists go so far as to suggest studies of human cultures will increasingly focus not on similarities between groups, but on their differences.

The lives of prehistoric Albertans can also teach the very art of human survival. The hunting and gathering way of life which they followed proved successful in almost all regions of the world, except Antarctica, for 40,000 years. Our modern industrial way of life is only a few hundred-years-old and has yet to establish its long-term viability. Occurrences such as the Chernobyl nuclear disaster cause many to question whether it ever will.

Archaeology and the Role of Volunteers

Archaeologists at the ASA occasionally receive unusual reports. Once, an individual called to say that he had unearthed pyramids in Alberta. Another call from northern Alberta alerted provincial archaeologists to what the caller believed to be the presence of giant beaver houses left by prehistoric beasts. Other callers routinely report the presence of flying saucers.

ASA

Crew of volunteers working on site at the Strathcona Archaeological Centre.

Such calls may be a nuisance, but they are in the minority. Many times, the alertness and willingness of amateur archaeologists to work with the ASA has resulted in a mutually beneficial relationship leading to important archaeological insights.

In an attempt to keep track of artifacts and facilitate smooth relationships between professional and amateur archaeologists, the ASA now offers a volunteer registration program. So far, between 500 to 600 collections have been registered, including fifty from the Grande Prairie area alone.

Too many times, though, the value of an artifact reported to professional archaeologists has been lost because the finder has made the cardinal error of removing it from its context. If you do come across artifacts which you think may be of archaeological significance, do not pack them into a shoebox. Instead, make a careful note of their exact location and, especially if they are in immediate danger, contact the ASA.

Despite damage done by some uninformed collectors, professional archaeologists are in general grateful for the role played by amateur archaeologists. Such rare sites as the Laidlaw Antelope Trap and the Ellis Medicine Wheel have been investigated by volunteers, members of the Archaeological Society of Alberta, who were willing to work in the boiling summer heat of southern Alberta under the direction of professional archaeologists. University students have also made important contributions to Alberta archaeology. One of the major gatherings of Canadian archaeologists, the Chacmool conference, is organized annually by the archaeological association of the University of Calgary.

Alberta Archaeology Tomorrow

The future does hold encouraging prospects for archaeology in this province. Archaeologists hope the interpretive centre at Head-Smashed-In Buffalo Jump near Fort Macleod will create an unprecedented level of public interest in the prehistory of Alberta. This ten million dollar facility, developed jointly by the Historic Sites Service and the ASA, is designed to explain the details of Indian use of buffalo jumps to tens of thousands of visitors annually.

Another ambitious research project is centred on the Eastern Slopes. Because key segments of the ice-free corridor lie within Alberta, investigations will contribute unique insights into the first human migrations into the Americas. There is, then, a sense in which Alberta has an international responsibility to discover if there really are traces of the passage of the first Native Americans along the foothills and front ranges of the Rockies.

Yet much more remains to be done in all archaeological zones in the province. On the plains, with the exception of Head-Smashed-In and Old Women's Buffalo Jump, few other bone beds at major bison jumps in Alberta have been excavated. Systematic archaeology in the boreal forest only began in the last fifteen years; historical archaeologists have only begun to study many of the fur trade sites of the north, and the early police forts and cattle ranches of southern Alberta.

Completing these studies with the limited manpower available will take years, perhaps decades. Yet, this research can only touch on the vast archaeological resources of a province so large it could swallow Great Britain two and a half times. In the meantime, the development of a personal sense of responsibility and custodianship is the best hope for preserving the story of Alberta's human past.

Crowfoot, chief of the Blackfoot, offered the following thought near his death:

> What is life? It is as the flash of a firefly in the night. It is as the breath of a buffalo in the wintertime. It is as the little shadow that runs across the grass and loses itself in the sunset . . .

That story must not be allowed to vanish like the flash of a firefly.

The Strathcona Archaeological Centre

Just a short drive from the centre of Edmonton, visitors can enter the world of 5,000 years ago. The curious can witness the on-going archaeological excavation of a prehistoric Native site, study replicas of prehistoric spears, bows and arrows and even try producing an arrow shaft. Guided tours through the excavation site are also available.

"The Strathcona site is the first archaeological site in Canada to offer, on a regular and formal basis, the opportunity for the public to observe, learn and participate in the scientific investigation of an archaeological site," says archaeologist Bruce Ball of the ASA.

The ASA funds a field school at the centre currently administered by the University of Calgary, which allows volunteers to spend weekends in archaeological work as well as to participate in a university field course. A Friends of Strathcona Archaeological Site society has been formed to coordinate volunteer efforts.

"The site is unique in providing the opportunity for volunteers, field-school students and research scientists, as well as the general public, to examine, learn and inquire about Alberta's prehistory," says Ball.

The Strathcona Archaeological Centre is operated by the ASA in conjunction with its sister branch, the Historic Sites Service. It is situated within Strathcona Science Park west of 17th St. between Highways 16 and 16A. Open Victoria Day to Labour Day.

Russell Johnston's Little Gem

Russell Johnston was not a man to give up easily — and Alberta archaeology is richer for his determination.

During the windy 1930s, the Excel, Alberta, resident noticed extensive erosion from drought had exposed several prehistoric artifacts nearby. Johnston tried to get a professional archaeologist to come to Alberta — there were few archaeologists around in those days, and virtually no funding available.

When he failed in that quest, Johnston instead took the task into his own hands, and began to collect artifacts systematically. Not only did he keep detailed location notes, but by returning to the sites periodically, he was able to collect material as lower and lower levels eroded. In this way, he was able to discover which artifacts had originally occurred together.

Johnston was the first person in Alberta to recognize that Eden and Scottsbluff points along with a distinctive knife style — the Cody knife — occurred together. He named this the Little Gem Complex, but, owing to prior publication, this is now known as the Cody Complex.

Johnston also found a point much like the Scottsbluff, but larger and with a longer stem. These points commonly occurred in sites also yielding Scottsbluff and Eden points. These points have been named Alberta points in honour of the province in which they were first recognized.

"Johnston is but one of many ordinary Albertans whose discoveries have advanced our knowledge," says Rod Vickers. "He is, however, unusual in that his extremely careful records and systematic approach resulted in a great deal more information than usual."

Postscript

The threads linking the present to the richness of the past are rather tenuous. In Alberta they are sometimes found in the delicate arrangements of stones on the landscape, or in a diffuse sprinkling of arrowheads along an eroding river bank. Such artifacts are irreplaceable and their value can easily be lost to scientists if they are not protected or are incorrectly removed from their context.

The *Alberta Historical Resources Act* protects archaeological resources by punishing persons who willfully destroy them with fines of up to $50,000, or a maximum of one year in prison. The legislation, enacted in 1973, has since served as a model for comparable legislation in other provinces. It also led to the establishment of the Archaeological Survey of Alberta, which is charged with protection and research of the province's archaeological heritage.

In reality, though, the protection of archaeological resources will not stem from harsh fines, but from the creation of an educated, responsible public.

"We can have all the legislation in the world, but it's not going to stop the pot-hunters," says Heather Devine, public education officer with the ASA. "The only way you can do that is by educating children about archaeology, and by making it accessible."

Devine, whose background is in education, not archaeology, devotes much of her time to visiting classrooms and meeting with members of the public who are interested in learning more about Alberta archaeology. She also lobbies for more emphasis on Alberta archaeology in the school curriculum.

The Social Studies program taught in Alberta schools ignores the existence of hunters and gatherers in the province for thousands of years. Students learn about ancient Greece, Rome and Meso-American civilizations to the exclusion of the Native hunter-gatherer culture in their own province. They are also denied the understanding which historic archaeology can give about ourselves and the fundamental social and economic forces which shaped Alberta's place in Canada, from the time of the fur trade through to the days of pioneers and early coal miners. Although few would argue for a narrow Alberta focus in our schools, such an information gap seems unjustifiable given the amount of interest in the subject and the rich amount of archaeological information available.

"Teachers are fascinated by archaeology; the kids are fascinated by archaeology, but quite often there aren't enough Alberta materials," Devine points out.

One glaring omission is now being corrected under the Native Learning Resources Project. A series of books focussing on Native peoples of Alberta is being produced for Grades One through Seven, following a provincial report on Native people in the school curriculum. Archaeological information will help form the underpinnings of the project, since almost 11,000 years of Alberta's human history is comprised of the activities of Native people.

Alberta Archaeology and Industry

Hearteningly, many companies have displayed good corporate citizenship when dealing with sites of archaeological value, and well-defined working relationships have been established between the ASA and public sector developers such as Alberta Transportation and Alberta Environment. When the value of the Sibbald Creek site was recognized, for example, the provincial transportation department realigned the highway to avoid destroying deposits of archaeological value. Companies like Esso Resources have also been generous in funding research at places such as the Duckett site, near Cold Lake.

These relationships have been of mutual benefit; Melcor Developments Ltd. received national publicity when the Hawkwood site was discovered in their proposed housing subdivision. A temporary museum was constructed as part of their sales campaign. As well, Nova Corporation developed an innovative archaeological display in the lobby of their office tower in Calgary.

Custodianship of archaeological resources must be a shared task, involving public and private sectors as well as professional archaeologists. No one pretends that the responsibility for making astute choices is always easy, especially during times of rapid economic growth.

Yet such choices are certainly achievable. "The pipeline *can* miss the tipi ring," says Jack Ives.

Appendix

Archaeological Survey of Alberta

The Archaeological Survey of Alberta is responsible for regulating archaeological activities in the province. The survey, administered by the Historical Resources Division of Alberta Culture and employing twenty-two staff members, is composed of a research section and a resource management section. The research section initiates archaeological research, undertakes site interpretation and cultural resource management. Staff members assess development proposals, review archaeological permit applications, issue and supervise contracts and review permit reports. The research section also publishes theses, reports, edited volumes and annual reports. Through the education officer, the research section coordinates educational programs dealing with archaeology and gives assistance to the Department of Education in curriculum development concerning archaeology and Native prehistory.

The resource management section administers a referral system for private and government land development, designates historic, archaeological and palaeontological sites, and maintains site inventory data for prehistoric and historic archaeological sites.

For further information, call (403) 431-2300, or write to: Archaeological Survey of Alberta, 8820-112 Street, Edmonton, Alberta, T6G 2P8.

The Archaeological Society of Alberta

The Archaeological Society of Alberta was first formed in September, 1960, in Edmonton, and issued a charter under the *Societies Act* on February 7, 1975. Currently the Society has 190 members and four centres located in Calgary, Edmonton, Medicine Hat and Lethbridge.

Society members have been very active in recording and mapping archaeological sites, monitoring ongoing activities at these sites, and bringing actual and potential impacts to the attention of the Archaeological Survey of Alberta. For example, during 1985, members monitored the Saamis site in the Seven Persons Coulee in an attempt to preserve its natural state; maintained a rotating display at Fort Calgary; and, voted to support the development of the Medalta Potteries site in Medicine Hat.

Local chapters of the Archaeological Society conduct monthly meetings which include presentations on a variety of topics in the fields of archaeology and history. In addition, the Society holds annual meetings which are attended by professionals from throughout the province, and members participate in conferences sponsored by other archaeological groups. A selection of papers presented at the annual meetings and reports on other activities and sites of interest are published in the Society's *Alberta Archaeological Review*, printed twice a year. The Society has contributed to public awareness about archaeology with the publication of *Alberta Archaeology: Prospect and Retrospect*, in 1981.

Finally, Society members have been involved in preserving other facets of our natural environment, specifically through their representation on the Public Advisory Council on Non-Renewable Resources.

For more information, contact the Archaeological Society of Alberta, 8820 - 112 Street, Edmonton, Alberta, T6G 2P8. Phone: 431-2300.

Alberta Provincial Historic Sites and Museums

Head-Smashed-In Buffalo Jump, Highway 785, 20 km west of Fort Macleod. 10 a.m. - 10 p.m. daily in summer; 10 a.m. - 5 p.m. Thursday to Monday, September and October. Phone 553-2030 or 427-2022.

Strathcona Archaeological Centre, 1 km south of Highway 16 on 17th Street, Strathcona Country, East Edmonton. Open 10 a.m. - 6 p.m. daily, Victoria Day Weekend to June 30; noon to 8 p.m. daily, July 1 to Labour Day. Phone: 427-2022 or 427-9487.

Tyrrell Museum of Palaeontology, 6 km northwest of Drumheller. Open 9 a.m. - 9 p.m. seven days a week during summer; 9 a.m. - 5 p.m. Tuesday through Sunday the rest of the year. Phone 823-7707 or 294-1992.

Provincial Museum of Alberta, 12845 102 Ave., Edmonton. Open 10 a.m. - 8 p.m. seven days a week. Closed Dec. 25. 427-1730.

Ukrainian Cultural Heritage Village, 50 km east of Edmonton on Highway 16. Open 10 a.m. - 6 p.m. daily, Victoria Day Weekend to Labour Day; 10 a.m. - 4 p.m. daily, Labour Day to Thanksgiving Weekend; 10 a.m. - 4 p.m. Monday to Friday for the remainder of the year. 662-3640, 421-7065 or 427-2022.

Frank Slide Interpretive Centre, Crowsnest Pass, north side of Highway 3. Open 10 a.m. - 8 p.m. daily, Victoria Day Weekend to Labour Day; 10 a.m. - 4 p.m. daily, for the rest of the year. Phone: 562-7388 or 427-2022.

Fort McMurray Oil Sands Interpretive Centre, Highway 63 at MacKenzie Blvd., Fort McMurray. Open 10 a.m. - 6 p.m. daily, Victoria Day Weekend to Labour Day; noon to 5 p.m. for the rest of the year. Phone: 743-7166 for 24-hour information or 743-2167 or 427-2022.

Alberta Natural Resources Science Centre, 1 km south of Highway 16 on 17th Street, Strathcona County, East Edmonton. Open 10 a.m. - 6 p.m. daily, Victoria Day Weekend to June 30; noon to 8 p.m. daily, July 1 to Labour Day Weekend; 11 a.m. - 5 p.m. Sundays, Labour Day to Victoria Weekend.

Rutherford House, 11153 Saskatchewan Dr., University of Alberta Campus, Edmonton. Open 10 a.m. - 6 p.m. daily, Victoria Day Weekend to Labour Day; noon to 5 p.m. daily, for the rest of the year. Phone: 427-3995 or 427-2022.

Stephansson House, off Highway 592 or 781 southwest of Red Deer. Open 10 a.m. - 6 p.m. daily, Victoria Day Weekend to Labour Day. Phone: 427-2022 or 728-3929.

Dunvegan, off Highway 2 beside Dunvegan bridge, north side of Peace River. Open 10 a.m. - 6 p.m. daily, Victoria Day Weekend to June 30; 10 a.m. - 9 p.m. daily, July 1 to Labour Day. Booked tours only from September 2 to 30. Phone: 835-4889 or 427-2022.

Cochrane Ranche, 1 km west of Cochrane near junction of Highways 22 and 1A. Open 10 a.m. - 8 p.m. daily, Victoria Day Weekend to Labour Day. Phone: 932-3242, 932-2902 or 427-2022.

Leitch Collieries, Crowsnest Pass, north side of highway 3. Open 10 a.m. - 6 p.m. daily, Victoria Day Weekend to Labour Day. Phone: 562-7388 or 427-2022.

Father Lacombe Chapel, St. Vital Avenue off St. Albert Trail, St. Albert. Open 10 a.m. - 6 p.m. daily, Victoria Day Weekend to Labour Day. Phone: 427-2022.

Victoria Settlement, off highway 855, 15 km south of Smoky Lake. Open 10 a.m. - 6 p.m. daily, Victoria Day weekend to Labour day. Phone: 662-3640, 421-7065 or 427-2022.

All sites offer visitor services and guided tours. Donations. For more information, call 1-800-222-6501 in Alberta; 1-800-661-8888 Canada and continental U.S.

Historical Societies of Alberta

Alberta Historical Society
c/o Mrs. Donna Coulter, President
Box 1001, Fort Macleod
T0L 0Z0
553-4369

Altamont Historical Centre
Box 176, Coutts
T0K 0N0

Archaeological Society of Alberta
P.O. Box 4609, Station C
Calgary T2T 5P1

- Calgary Centre
2510 21 St. SW
Calgary T2T 5A8

- Lethbridge Centre
306 23 St. South
Lethbridge T1S 3M6

- Edmonton Centre
5811 113A St.
Edmonton T6H 1A9

- Medicine Hat Centre
35 Garden Place, NW
Medicine Hat T1A 1R3

Big Valley Historical Society
c/o Mr. Allen Johnston
Box 40, Big Valley
T0J 0G0
876-2593

Bonnyville Historical Society
Box 2502, Bonnyville
T0A 0L0
826-4240

Breton and District Historical Society
Box 423, Breton
T0C 0P0

Cochrane Area Heritage Association
Box 1063, Cochrane
T0L 0W0

Deville-North Cooking
Lake Historical Society
General Delivery
North Cooking Lake
T0B 3N0

Duhamel Historical
Society
c/o Mr. Stan Trautman
R.R. 1, New Norway
T0B 3L0
855-2280

Fort Saskatchewan
Historical Society
10104 101 Street
Fort Saskatchewan
T8L 1V9

Friends of Head-Smashed-In
Buffalo Jump
P.O. Box 1977
Fort Macleod T0L 0Z0

Heritage Franco-Albertain
Box 3078, St. Paul
T0A 3A0
645-4410

Hinton and District
Historical Foundation
Box 2355, Hinton
T0E 1C0

Kneehill Historical
Society
Box 653, Three Hills
T0M 2A0

Medicine Hat Historical
and Museum Foundation
132 Bomford Crescent SW
Medicine Hat T1A 5E6
527-6266

Millet Historical Society
Box 178, Millet
T0C 1Z0

Morinville Historical
and Cultural Centre
Box 57, T0G 1P0
939-2955

Neerlandia Historical
Society
c/o Mrs. Karen Mast
Box 150 Neerlandia
T0G 1R0
674-4020

Nordegg Historic Heritage
Interest Group
Box 2039
Rocky Mountain House
T0M 1T0
845-2229

Redcliff Museum and
Historical Society
Box 76, Redcliff
T0J 2P0
548-6260

Société Historique et
Généologique de Smoky
River
General Delivery
Donnelly T0H 1G0
925-3801

Strathcona Archaeological
Society
8820 112 St.
Edmonton T6G 2P8

Strathcona County
Heritage Foundation
c/o Sheila Abercrombie
169 Great Oak
Sherwood Park
T8A 0Z8

Strome Museum
Historical Society
Box 94, Strong
T0B 4H0

Sundre and District
Historical Society
Box 264, Sundre T0M 1X0
638-3233

Taber and District
Museum Society
Box 189, Taber T0K 2G0

Trochu Valley Historical
Society
Box 56, Trochu T0M 2C0
442-2334

Underwater Archaeological
Society of Alberta
13174 114 Ave.
Edmonton
T5M 2Y2

Whitecourt and District
Historical Society
c/o John Dahl
4832 53 Ave., Whitecourt
T0E 2L0
778-2864

Museums of Alberta

Alberta Beach Museum
Alberta Beach T0E 0A0

Altamont Museum
P.O. Box 176
Coutts T0K 0N0

Andrew and District
Local History Museum
P.O. Box 180
Andrew T0B 0C0

Anthony Henday Museum
P.O. Box 374, Delburne
T0M 0V0

Archives of the
Canadian Rockies
P.O. Box 160, Banff
T0L 0C0

Banff National Park
Natural History Museum
P.O. Box 900, Banff
T0L 0C0

Barrhead and District
Centennial Museum
P.O. Box 626, Barrhead
T0G 0E0

Brooks and District
Museum
P.O. Box 2078, Brooks
T0J 0J0

Calgary Zoo
Botanical Gardens and
Prehistoric Park
P.O. Box 3036, St. B
Calgary T2M 4R8

Camrose and District
Centennial Museum
20 Grand Park Crescent
Camrose T4V 2K3

Castor and District
Museum
P.O. Box 92, Castor
T0C 0X0

Cereal Prairie
Pioneer Museum
P.O. Box 131, Cereal
T0J 0N0

Claresholm Museum
P.O. Box 1000
Claresholm
T0L 0T0

Crossroads Museum
P.O. Box 477, Oyen
T0J 2J0

Debolt and District Pioneer Museum
Debolt T0H 1B0

Dinosaur Provincial Park
General Delivery
Patricia T0J 2K0

Drumheller and District Fossil Museum
P.O. Box 2135
Drumheller
T0J 0Y0

Fort Calgary
P.O. Box 2100
Calgary
T2P 2M5

Fort Edmonton Park
Edmonton Parks and
Recreation
10th Flr., CN Tower
Edmonton
T5J 0K1

Fort George Museum
P.O. Box 66, Elk Point
T0A 1A0

Fort Ostell Museum
P.O. Box 2192, Ponoka
T0C 2H0

Fort Saskatchewan
10104 101 St.
Fort Saskatchewan
T8L 1V9

Fort Whoop-Up
P.O. Box 1074
Lethbridge T1J 4A2

Frontier Memorial Museum
P.O. Box 186
Duchess T0J 0Z0

Glenbow Museum
130 9th Ave., SE
Calgary T2G 0P3

Hanna Pioneer Museum
P.O. Box 1528, Hanna
T0J 1P0

Heritage Village
25 Crescent Heights
Fort McMurray T9H 1L6

High Prairie and District Centennial Museum
P.O. Box 642, Innisfail
T0M 1A0

Iron Creek Museum
P.O. Box 6, Lougheed
T0B 2V0

Kinnoull Historical Museum
General Delivery
Colinton
T0G 0K0

Lac Ste. Anne and District Pioneer Museum
P.O. Box 186
Sangudo
T0E 2A0

Luxton Museum
1 Birch Ave.
Banff T0L 0C0

Medicine Hat Museum and Art Gallery
1302 Bomford Crescent SW
Medicine Hat
T1A 5E6

Mountain View Museum
P.O. Box 63, Olds
T0M 1P0

**Multicultural Heritage
Centre**
P.O. Box 908, Stony Plain
T0E 2G0

Musée Girouxville
C.P. 129, Girouxville
T0H 1S0

Musée Historique de St. Paul
C.P. 1925, St. Paul
T0A 3A0

Museum of the Highwood
P.O. Box 456, High River
T0L 1B0

**Plamondon and
District Museum**
Plamondon T0A 2T0

Pas-Ka-Poo Historical Park
Rimbey T0C 2J0

**Peace River
Centennial Museum**
P.O. Box 747
Peace River T0H 2X0

**Pembina Lobstick
Historical Museum**
Evansburg T0E 0T0

Pincher Creek Museum
P.O. Box 1226
Pincher Creek
T0K 1W0

**Pioneer Museum Society
of Grande Prairie**
P.O. Box 687
Grande Prairie
T3V 3A8

Prairie Memories Museum
General Delivery
Irvine T0J 1V0

Prairie Panorama Museum
P.O. Box 156, Czar T0B 0Z0

**Provincial Museum of
Alberta**
12845 102 Ave.
Edmonton T5N 0M6

**Rainy Hills
Pioneer Exhibits**
Iddesleigh T0J 1T0

**Red Deer and District
Museum and Archives**
P.O. Box 762
Red Deer T4N 5H2

Redwater Museum
Redwater T0A 2W0

**Rocky Lake
School Museum**
P.O. Box 184
Fort Vermilion T0H 1H0

**Rocky Mountain House
National Historic Park**
P.O. Box 2130
Rocky Mountain House
T0M 1T0

**Rosebud Centennial
Museum**
P.O. Box 667, Rosebud
T0J 2T0

**Sir Alexander Galt
Museum and Archives**
Community Services
Department
City of Lethbridge
Lethbridge T1J 0P6

**South Peace
Centennial Museum**
P.O. Box 493
Beaverlodge T0H 0C0

St. Albert Place Museum
5 St. Anne St.
St. Albert T8N 1E8

**Stettler Town and Country
Museum**
P.O. Box Box 2118
Stettler T0C 2L0

**Sundre and District
Historical Society Museum**
Sundre T0M 1X0

The Fort Museum
P.O. Box 776
Fort Macleod T0L 0Z0

Tofield Historical Museum
Tofield T0B 4J0

**Tyrrell Museum of
Palaeontology**
P.O. Box 7500
Drumheller T0J 0Y0

Viking Historical Museum
P.O. Box 232
Viking T0B 4N0

**Wagon Wheel Regional
Museum**
P.O. Box 157
Alix T0C 0B0

Wainwright Museum
P.O. Box 1315
Wainwright
T0B 4P0

Glossary

Compiled by the Archaeological Survey of Alberta

A

ACASTA: Acasta Lake Complex and Acasta Lake Site. Archaeological complex defined in area of Great Slave Lake of the Northwest Territories dating to 5,000 years before present.

A.D.: *Anno domini* in Latin. "In the year of our Lord." For example, A.D. 1950 is 1950 years since Christ.

AGATE BASIN POINT: Large lanceolate spear points employed approximately 10,500 to 10,000 years ago. It has been suggested that these points were used even more recently in areas as far north as the Northwest Territories.

ALBERTA POINT: Large spear points used about 9,500 to 8,900 years ago. Named in honour of the province by Russell Johnson, an avocational archaeologist. They are grouped into the Cody Complex along with Scottsbluff and Eden points.

ALTITHERMAL: Prolonged period of time in the mid-Holocene when temperatures were warmer and in some areas, conditions may also have been drier than today. Occurred approximately between 9,000 and 4,000 years ago.

ANTHROPOLOGY: The study of the human species, our ancestors, and our closest living relatives, the great apes and monkeys. Consists of four sub-disciplines: (1) Archaeology, the study of the human past. (2) Cultural anthropology, the study of living human groups. (3) Physical anthropology, the study of human physical evolution and adaptation. (4) Linguistics, the study of human languages.

ARCHAEOLOGY: The study of the human past, not to be confused with palaeontology, the study of fossil remains. Archaeology can also include the study of contemporary material culture including forensic investigation at crime scenes.

ARTIFACT: Any item made or modified by human means.

ASSEMBLAGE: The entire collection of artifacts or bones found at an archaeological site. Artifacts recovered from the same time period represent a component.

ATLATL: A short board or stick, forty-five to sixty centimetres long, fitted with a handle on one end and a groove or peg at the other end, used for throwing a dart or light spear. Extends arm's leverage. Likely used in Middle Prehistoric period.

AVONLEA: Avonlea points are small and finely made. They mark the appearance of the bow and arrow in the province about 1,750 to 1,150 years ago. The Avonlea Complex shows the first use of pottery vessels—simple, coconut-shaped pots.

AWL: A tool used to make a hole in leather or hide which is too tough to pierce with a needle. The holes produced were then used for sewing. Prehistoric awls are usually sharply-pointed bone items.

B

B.C.: Before Christ, as opposed to B.P. or A.D. With the A.D. 1950 convention, a radiocarbon date of 3,000 B.C. equals 4950 B.P.

BERINGIA: Extended from the Kolyma River in the Soviet Union to the Mackenzie River in Canada. It included much of eastern Siberia and Alaska, the Yukon, and part of the Northwest Territories, together with adjacent shallow continental shelf areas where the water depth is less than 150 metres.

BESANT: A widespread cultural phase dating generally 2,000 to 1,000 years ago and using a characteristic style of side-notched atlatl point which was first recognized in Saskatchewan. It is the final phase of the Middle Prehistoric period and likely underwent major transformation with the introduction of bow and arrow weaponry. Its origins are unclear, but certain material and cultural traits suggest some connections with Middle Missouri drainage agricultural societies.

BIFACE: Stone artifact formed by flaking or chipping on both sides or faces. Refers to a wide variety of stone tools. Projectile points, drills and knives are most often bifacially flaked.

BIRCH MOUNTAINS: A remnant of the Alberta Plateau. This upland area in the northeast quadrant of the province is covered by mixed wood and boreal forest. Largely composed of poorly drained organic soils.

BOREAL: Northern. From the Greek—Boreas, god of north wind.

B.P.: Before Present. Used to denote time, commonly in reference to radiocarbon dates, for example, 2500 ± 200 years B.P. By international convention, "Present" is A.D. 1950. This is because fossil fuels and nuclear tests have introduced significant changes in C14 content in the atmosphere.

BUFFALO POUND: A corral with a funnel-shaped fence leading to the entrance. Small herds of buffalo could be driven into the pound and killed. Usually made of brush and hides.

C

CHERT: A particular type of very fine-grained homogeneous stone suitable for chipping into stone tools. Its usage is often synonymous with the term flint in North America. The principal mineral is silica (SiO_2). The rock occurs as outcrops or as pebbles and cobbles in stream and glacial till deposits.

CLOVIS: A large spear point with grooves or "flutes" from the base to about one half the length of the point. Used between 11,500 and 11,000 years ago to hunt mammoths. The point type may have been introduced by the first people to enter the New World.

CODY COMPLEX: Named after Cody, Wyoming. A group of sites dating 9,500 to 8,300 years ago. Alberta, Scottsbluff and Eden points occur in Cody Complex sites as do peculiarly-shaped knives of the same name.

COMPLEX: A group of sites dating from the same time period and containing similar artifacts. Origins, descendants and other details are not yet known. Used to express a relationship of common cultural or technological traits in assemblages with a widespread, usually contiguous, geographic area, and often of considerable temporal duration. *See also* PHASE.

CORDILLERA: A mountain range or chain. Often employed as a general term referring to the mountain ranges of Western Canada.

CORNER-NOTCHED: Refers to notches made obliquely into the two bottom corners of some projectile points, such as Pelican Lake and Oxbow types.

CRETACEOUS: Geological period before the Tertiary, lasting from about 135 to 65 million years ago.

D

DEBITAGE: A French word for the detritus or leftover debris that represent waste of stone tool manufacture. Its usage here usually refers to stone waste flakes and shatter.

DIFFUSION: The spread of characteristics, items or groups from one place to others.

E

EASTERN WOODLANDS: Refers to ancient cultures of the forests of eastern North America. People of the Eastern Woodlands hunted deer and small game, began intensive agriculture about the time of Christ, and buried their dead in mounds. By about A.D. 700, they had established towns with pyramid-shaped temple mounds grouped around a central plaza.

ETHNOGRAPHY: The collection of contemporary cultural and social information. An anthropological discipline.

F

FLAKE: Waste item of chipped stone tool manufacture, or debitage. Also bone flakes, resulting from smashing up bone; thin flat piece.

FLESHER: A blunt bone or stone tool used to remove and scrape flesh and fat from the inner surface of animal hides.

FLUTED: Flutes, fluting, fluted points. Some stone projectile points have single or few large flakes or flutes removed from bases to facilitate attachment to wood or bone shafts. *See also* CLOVIS *and* FOLSOM.

FOLSOM: Names after Folsom, New Mexico, the first place where, in 1926, a fluted point style was found with extinct buffalo. These points date to around 11,000 - 10,500 B.P.

G

GRAVE GOODS: Artifacts deposited with the dead. They may be personal property of the deceased or offerings by mourners.

H

HEARTH: The location of a campfire. Such areas were on the ground surface sometimes surrounded by rocks to contain the fire, or the earth was scooped out to form a shallow basin where the fire was built. Archaeologists recognize hearths by the presence of ash and charcoal, as well as by red-stained soil formed by heat from the fire.

HISTORICAL ARCHAEOLOGY: The study of the historic (written history) period, drawing upon written, oral and archaeological evidence.

HOLOCENE: The youngest Epoch in geologic terminology. Equivalent to the last 10,000 years. Together with the Pleistocene Epoch, it makes up the Quarternary Period.

K

KARST: Terrain with irregular topography and a distinctive assemblage of landforms, including sinkholes, streamless valleys, streams disappearing underground, and often complex underground conduits and caverns. These features are formed by the action of surface and underground water on soluble rock, principally limestone.

KILL SITES: The locations where animals were killed. They consist primarily of discarded bones resulting from the initial stages of butchering. Varying widely in their locations and contents, they can represent the remains of a single animal or repetitive incidents involving small herds, which resulted in massive deposits of bone and associated butchering tools. Studies of these sites are especially valuable for understanding prehistoric subsistence strategies. Archaeological evidence at these sites usually consists of the undesirable portions of the animals as well as artifacts used for killing and butchering.

KNOLL: A small hill or mound.

L

LAURENTIDE ICE SHEET: A vast ice mass centered on the Canadian Shield. At its maximum extent the ice covered most of Canada east of the Rocky Mountains.

LIMESTONE: A sedimentary rock composed of calcium carbonate.

LITHIC: "Of Stone." This term, when used by archaeologists, refers to stone artifacts whether they are tools or debitage. As opposed to "ceramic" meaning "of clay."

M

MAMMOTH: A large, elephant-like beast common during the Pleistocene Epoch. The woolly mammoth (*Mammuthus primigenius*) portrayed in European cave paintings inhabited the tundra and spruce forest of Eurasia and North America. Entire frozen carcasses have been discovered. Mammoths stood two to three metres high at the shoulder, and had a high, domed head, humped, sloping back and short trunk. Another larger species (*Mammuthus columbi*) inhabited the plains south of the ice. Both types of mammoth have been found in early kill sites in the United States and were extinct by about 11,000 years ago.

MASTODON: Large, elephant-like mammals of the Pleistocene Epoch (*mammut americanum*). More heavily built than mammoths, they stood almost three metres high at the shoulder and primarily inhabited open spruce and pine woodlands of North America. They became extinct between 12,000 and 9,000 years ago.

MEGAFAUNA: The term means "large animals," but has come to refer to the now-extinct animals of the Ice Age. Before about 12,000 years ago, a host of large animals could be found in North America. These included mammoth, mastodon, giant sloths, giant wolves, sabre-tooth and lion-like cats, giant bison and beaver. Only a few species of these animals, such as the bison, survive today.

MICROBLADE: Long, narrow flake, at least twice as long as wide, with parallel sides, approximately three to six millimetres wide and ten to thirty millimetres long. Struck from specially prepared cores. (Larger specimens are called blades or macroblades.) Microblades are poorly represented in Alberta, but are thought to date to ca. 5,000 years B.P. Some in Alberta may date to the Early Prehistoric Period.

MICROCORE: Parent piece from which microblades are removed.

MIGRATION: The movement of groups.

MUMMY CAVE COMPLEX: A series of archaeological components characterized by the use of large side-notched stone points which were first recognized in a cave site in Wyoming. This complex may represent the introduction of the atlatl, or spear thrower, into Alberta. Dating between 8,000 and 5,000 years ago, Mummy Cave occupations correspond to the Altithermal climatic maximum.

N

NORTHERN PLAINS: The plains area of Wyoming, Montana, North and South Dakota, Alberta, Saskatchewan and Manitoba. Except for farming villages along the Missouri River, peoples of the Northern Plains made their living by hunting, especially the buffalo.

O

OBSIDIAN: An extremely sharp volcanic glass occurring naturally in British Columbia, Oregon, Wyoming, California and Alaska. This stone is highly valued for stone tool manufacture and was traded into Alberta.

OLD WOMEN'S PHASE: Named after a buffalo jump near Cayley, sites of this phase contain small side-notched arrowheads and pottery. This phase dates from approximately 1,200 to 225 years ago.

OXBOW: Oxbow points are medium-sized, notched points used on darts thrown with an atlatl. They were used in Alberta between 5,000 and 3,500 years ago.

P

PALEO-INDIAN: A term for the cultures of the Early Prehistoric Period dating between 11,500 and 7,500 years ago. Includes Clovis, Folsom, Agate Basin, Hell Gap, Alberta/Cody, and the terminal complexes of that period.

PEACE POINT: A deeply stratified archaeological site on the lower reaches of the Peace River in northeastern Alberta. Two metres of sedimentary deposit contain eighteen layers of campsite debris spanning the time from 2,500 years ago to present.

PELICAN LAKE: Pelican Lake points are medium-sized dart points which were used between about 3,300 and 2,000 years ago. The points are corner-notched with barb-like shoulders.

PETROGLYPH: Rock art produced by a subtractive proces such as pecking or incising a rock surface.

PHASE: A group of related assemblages containing similar cultural material and dating to a relatively narrow time period. Sites in a phase are the remains of activities conducted by people of one cultural group; phases can be linked through time into a tradition. *See also* COMPLEX.

PICTOGRAPH: Rock art produced by an additive process such as the application of paint or ochre on a rock surface.

PLEISTOCENE: The penultimate Epoch in stratigraphic terminology. Sometimes called the Age of Glaciation. The beginning of the Pleistocene is generally considered to be about two million years ago. Together with the Holocene Epoch, it makes up the Quaternary Period.

POLLEN ANALYSIS: The identification of pollen grains and the interpretation of the resulting data in terms of the surrounding vegetation and environment. Pollen grains, which may be preserved in vast numbers in lake sediments and bog deposits, are often identified according to the plants from which they came. Pollen analysis is a major technique for investigating environments in the Holocene.

PRINCIPLE OF SUPERPOSITION: This fundamental geological principle states that in any sequence of sedimentary rocks or other surface deposited material such as till, which has not been disturbed or deformed, each bed (layer) is younger than the one below it and older than the one above it.

PROJECTILE POINT: Refers to all weapon tips and includes large spear points, medium-sized dart points and small arrowheads. Large projectile points (spearheads) are typical of the Early Prehistoric Period (11,500 - 7,500 years ago), medium-sized projectile points (dartheads) are typical of the Middle Prehistoric Period (7,500 - 2,000 years ago), and small projectile points (arrowheads) are typical of the Late Prehistoric Period (2,000 - 250 years ago).

PROTOHISTORIC: Period immediately preceding the written historic period in any region. A period of indirect contact between Native groups and European civilization. For example, in many parts of North America, metal goods were traded among Native groups in advance of actual European arrival.

R

RADIOCARBON DATING: The estimation of the age of organic material by measuring the radioactive isotope carbon-14, which is a natural component of the tissues of all living material. C-14 loses half its radioactivity in about 5,570 years following the death of the organism. Specimens less than about 40,000-years-old can be reliably dated with varying degrees of precision.

ROCK ART: Petroglyphs or pictographs producing design elements that may convey symbolism or depict actual historical events.

S

SCOTTSBLUFF: Large stemmed spear points used between about 8,800 to 8,300 years ago. Scottsbluff, Eden and Alberta points are grouped into the Cody Complex.

SCRAPER: A tool rather like a plane employed to scrape hide, wood or bone. The bit end or working edge may be transverse to (endscraper) or parallel with (sidescraper) the long axis of the tool. Fine quality stone, often imported, was commonly selected to make both endscrapers and projectile points.

SIDE-NOTCHED: Notches on the side of a projectile point holding the sinew binding which attached the point of the arrow or dart shaft. Prairie and plains side-notched points are arrow points used in the Old Women's Phase.

STEMMED: Refers to the shape of bases of particular projectile points such as Alberta and Scottsbluff.

STRATIGRAPHY: The study of stratified rocks, including their formation, character, age, distribution, and correlation.

STRATIFICATION: Layering caused by deposition of sediments in layers.

SUCCESSION: A sequence of changes in vegetation. For example, following a fire, aspen poplar may grow first, then gradually spruce invades the site and the aspen dies out.

T

TERTIARY: Period before the Quaternary. Together, the Tertiary and Quaternary Periods make up the Cenozoic Era. The Tertiary lasted roughly from sixty-five to two million years ago.

TIPI: A portable dwelling made from animal hides. The use of tipis as dwellings is characteristic of Middle and Late Prehistoric Periods.

TIPI RINGS: Circular arrangement of stones anchoring the hide covering of a tipi. When the tipi was removed, rocks were left behind marking the actual location where the tipi was placed. Found throughout the Alberta grasslands, they vary widely in size, location and in the amount of associated cultural remains.

TYPOLOGY: The study of types of artifacts by means of classification and analysis of particular characteristics of specimens.

Bibliography

Bicchieri, W.G., ed. *Hunters and Gatherers Today*. New York: Holt, Reinhart and Winston, Inc., 1972.

Boas, Franz. *The Central Eskimo*. Lincoln: University of Nebraska Press, 1888.

Brink, Jack. *Dog Days in Southern Alberta*. Archaeological Survey of Alberta, Occasional Paper no. 28. Edmonton: Alberta Culture, Historical Resources Division, 1986.

Brown, Jennifer S. *Strangers in Blood*. Vancouver: University of British Columbia Press, 1980.

Caldwell, Warren, ed. *The Northwestern Plains: A Symposium*. Billings: The Centre for Indian Studies, 1968.

Cooper, Dave, and Andrew Ogle. "Ancestors." Edmonton: The Edmonton Journal, 1986.

Epp, Henry T., and Ian Dyck. *Tracking Ancient Hunters*. Regina: Saskatchewan Archaeological Society, 1983.

Forbis, Richard G. *A Review of Alberta Archaeology to 1964*. Ottawa: National Museum of Canada, 1970.

Forbis, Richard G., and W.C. Noble. "Archaeology." *The Canadian Encyclopedia*. Vol. 1, 71-73. Edmonton: Hurtig Publishers, 1985.

Forsman, Michael R.A., and Sheila J. Minni. *Archaeological Investigations: Writing-On-Stone N.W.M.P. Post*. Archaeological Survey of Alberta, Occasional Paper no. 4. Edmonton: Alberta Culture, Historical Resources Division, 1977.

Forsman, Michael R.A., *The Archaeology of Victoria Post, 1864 - 1897*. Archaeological Survey of Alberta, Occasional Paper no. 6. Edmonton: Alberta Culture, Historical Resources Division, 1985.

Frison, George C. *Prehistoric Hunters of the High Plains*. New York: Academic Press, Inc., 1978.

Getty, Ronald M., and Knut Fladmark. *Historical Archaeology in Northwestern North America*. Calgary: University of Calgary Archaeological Association, 1973.

Goudie, Andrew, *Environmental Change*. Oxford: Oxford University Press, 1977.

Heitzmann, Roderick J. *The Cochrane Ranche Site*. Archaeological Survey of Alberta, Occasional Paper no. 16. Edmonton: Alberta Culture, Historical Resources Division, 1980.

Ives, John W. *A Spatial Analysis of Artifact Distribution on a Boreal Forest Archaeological Site.* Archaeological Survey of Alberta, Manuscript Series no. 5. Edmonton: Alberta Culture, Historical Resources Division, 1985.

Karklins, Karlis. *Nottingham House: The Hudson's Bay Company in Athabasca 1802 - 1806.* Ottawa: Environment Canada, 1983.

Lee, Richard B., and Irven Devore. *Man the Hunter.* Chicago: Aldine, Atherton, 1968.

Losey, Timothy C., and Heinz W. Pyszczyk, eds. *Fort George Project Interim Report No. 2: Archaeological Investigations, 1978.* Edmonton: Department of Anthropology, University of Alberta, 1978.

Martin, Calvin. *Keepers of the Game.* Berkeley: University of California Press, 1978.

McGhee, Robert. "Prehistory." *The Canadian Encyclopedia.* Vol. 3, 1466-1469. Edmonton: Hurtig Publishers, 1985.

Moore, T.A., ed. *Alberta Archaeology: Prospect and Retrospect.* Lethbridge: The Archaeological Society of Alberta, 1981.

Nelson, Richard K. *Hunters of the Northern Forest.* Chicago and London: The University of Chicago Press, 1973.

Norman, Howard. *The Wishing Bone Cycle.* New York: Stonehill, 1976.

Reeves, Brian O.K. "Six Milleniums of Bison Kills." *Scientific American.* 249(4). 1983.

——.*Culture Change in the Northern Plains—1000 B.C. - A.D. 1000.* Archaeological Survey of Alberta, Occasional Paper no. 20. Edmonton: Alberta Culture, Historical Resources Division, 1983.

Stevenson, Marc G. *Window on the Past.* Archaeological Assessment of the Peace Point Site, Wood Buffalo National Park, Alberta. Ottawa: Environment Canada.

Vickers, J. Roderick. *Alberta Plains Prehistory: A Review.* Archaeological Survey of Alberta, Occasional Paper no. 27. Edmonton, Alberta Culture, Historical Resources Division, 1986.

Williams, Glyndwr. "The Hudson's Bay Company and the Fur Trade: 1670 - 1870." Winnipeg: The Beaver, 1983.

Wormington, H.M., and Richard G. Forbis, eds. *An Introduction to the Archaeology of Alberta, Canada.* Denver: Denver Museum of Natural History, 1965.

Wright J.V. *Six Chapters of Canada's Prehistory.* Ottawa: National Museum of Canada, 1976.

The Author

Gail Helgason is both an award-winning journalist and former editorial writer with *The Edmonton Journal*. Helgason is also the co-author of *Bicycle Alberta, The Canadian Rockies Bicycling Guide* and *The Canadian Rockies Access Guide*. She lives in Edmonton where she works as a freelance writer and editor.